Teaching Mathematics 7–13:
Slow Learning and Able Pupils

Edith Biggs

NFER-NELSON

Published by The NFER-NELSON Publishing Company Ltd.,
Darville House, 2 Oxford Road East,
Windsor, Berkshire SL4 1DF

First Published 1985
© Edith Biggs, 1985
ISBN 0 7005 0661 6
Code 8178 02 1

Photoset in Baskerville by Illustrated Arts Ltd
Printed by Billing & Sons Ltd., Worcester, Worcestershire

Distributed in the USA by Taylor and Francis Inc.,
242 Cherry Street,
Philadelphia, PA 19106 – 1906
Tel: (215) 238 0939. Telex: 244489.

Contents

CHAPTER FOUR Activities used with slow learners
(aged 10 to 12) and some of their responses

CHAPTER FIVE Conclusions from the project and some
recommendations for work in mathematics with slow learners

CHAPTER SIX Activities used with able children at first
schools and some of their responses

CHAPTER SEVEN Activities used with able children aged
8 to 10 at middle schools and some of their responses

CHAPTER EIGHT Activities used with able third and
fourth years at middle schools and some of their responses

Foreword

This book describes work undertaken by some exceptional children: some who found mathematics very difficult to learn and others who found it easy and exciting. Several of their teachers found these children difficult to teach. I hope that all those who teach children from 5 to 13 will find the contents of the book both relevant to their own work and a useful source of ideas.

Some of the activities involve mathematics which may be unfamiliar to teachers. In these instances I have inserted notes on the mathematical concepts which underlie the work. Some of the activities may also be unfamiliar, particularly those described in Chapter Eight.

The best way of understanding the development of the mathematical ideas is to work through any unfamiliar activities yourself, using the material described. You will then understand the children's reactions and my subsequent questioning, which is directed to helping them to take the next step forward. You will also be prepared for any difficulties which may arise when you ask children to undertake these activities in your classroom. I hope you will enjoy them as much as I did.

I should like to thank all the children (as well as their teachers) for cooperating willingly and for helping me to understand the different ways in which some children can learn mathematics. I also appreciated their honest and sometimes critical comments on the activities we undertook.

I should like to give my warmest thanks to Mrs. Dora Whittaker for communicating to me and to many other teachers her own enthusiasm for mathematics – and for showing us the exhilarating mathematics which children could learn with an inspiring teacher.

Finally I thank Miss Kay Burton for helping me to say what I wanted to say. I appreciate her expertise with language.

Introduction

For many years teachers of children up to the age of 13 years have been particularly worried by the problems of doing justice to both the slow-learning children and the able ones in large classes. Although the number of children in a class is now considerably lower than in the 1960s the problem of exceptional children remains as difficult to solve as ever.

In my career as a secondary teacher of mathematics I was always interested in children at both ends of the ability range. I was fortunate enough to be able to try different ways of teaching for two lengthy periods:

(1) when I carried out research into why girls find mathematics difficult;
(2) when I introduced an integrated mathematics syllabus (instead of arithmetic, algebra and geometry) for pupils aged 11 to 16.

I found that it was possible for pupils to learn mathematics by means of investigations (sometimes using materials) and questioning, rather than by demonstration and practice, the method by which I myself was taught at school. The immediate positive effect of giving pupils an opportunity to investigate a new topic and to develop their own solutions (in other words, giving them more responsibility for their own learning of mathematics) took me completely by surprise. They developed an enthusiasm for mathematics and no longer asked: 'Why do we have to learn mathematics? Will it be any use to us when we leave school?' and (worse) 'Is it in the syllabus?' Although I was introducing new material no one checked it against the examination syllabus. Even those pupils who had previously shown no interest made great efforts to arrive at original solutions. For the first time they began to develop investigations further and to create mathematics for themselves.

When later on, as HMI, I worked with children at the primary phase, I found that here, too, children's interest was captured if they were given real problems to solve and the necessary material was available to help them to arrive at a solution. By means of carefully structured activities and discussion, they were able to acquire and understand mathematical concepts. Neither did they need to be shown methods of calculation; these, too, could be developed through activities and questioning, provided that the children had an adequate knowledge of number facts. Gradually I spent more of my time in infant and junior schools, working with teachers and children. I began to specialize in mathematics and eventually I was given national responsibility for helping teachers at this level with their teaching of mathematics. In consequence I spent a good deal of time on in-service education in mathematics, running initial and follow-up workshops in this subject. I also spent time in classrooms observing teachers trying new work and frequently joining them in their experiments. But I realized that although mathematics workshops created enthusiasm and caused teachers to begin to change the emphasis of their mathematics teaching, many of them gradually lost the initial impetus when they came to the end of their mathematical resources. Something else was required to sustain the changes teachers had begun to make.

By the time I retired in October 1974 I had become acutely aware of the relatively small amount of permanent change which resulted from initial and follow-up workshops. I therefore planned a research project on in-service education in mathematics. The input would include not only workshops but also support for individual teachers in their classrooms while they were implementing changes. I would be at hand when they felt at a loss in trying to plan the next step in the development of a topic. This process gave me further experience in working with children in a more continuous way than when I was HMI.

During the project an opportunity arose for me to carry out sustained work with groups of children from every project school. There was an interval of two terms between the first and second inputs of both working sessions and support visits. During this interval I wanted to leave the teachers free to plan their own activities and to try these in their classrooms. On the other hand, I wanted to maintain contact with the schools so that I could unobtrusively monitor the progress being made. In my first interviews with the teachers I had asked them to identify children who caused them teaching problems. I was surprised to find that many teachers first mentioned specially able children. One teacher said: 'John streaks ahead and always finishes long before anyone else. I find it hard to keep him occupied. There are not enough examples in any book.'

Of course the teachers also mentioned slow-learning children (and some disturbed children, too) as those causing problems. I therefore decided to work with both slow learners and able children nominated by the teachers. I appreciated the problems with which these exceptional children presented their teachers. I wanted to encounter the difficulties at first hand, without being faced by problems of control arising from large numbers. I therefore worked with groups of these children (with a two-year age range, so that all of the twelve project schools could be included) over a period of two terms.

This book comprises an account of my work with these groups of children over two terms, together with examples of children's work undertaken in cooperation with a teacher some years ago.

CHAPTER ONE

The framework of the experiment

I. Background

The opportunity of working in a sustained way with groups of slow-learning children and able ones arose during an action research project which I began in 1976. Throughout the 20 years I spent trying to help primary teachers to improve their teaching of mathematics I had found that mathematics workshops alone were insufficient to have a permanent effect on the teaching of mathematics at that phase. I therefore planned to investigate the effects of in-service education comprising both working sessions and support visits to schools to help individual teachers to consolidate the changes initiated by the mathematics workshops. From previous experience I had also learned that one input of in-service education would not be enough to sustain the initial impetus given. Consequently, I planned two inputs of both working sessions and support visits, with an interval of two terms between these inputs. It was during this interval that I organized regular visits to the twelve first and middle schools to work with groups of slow learning and of able children.

My major purpose was to experience, at first hand, some of the problems encountered by the teachers when they were attempting to introduce new content and to change the style of their teaching of mathematics. Every teacher had some children who found mathematics difficult, as well as the one or two who raced ahead and completed the work set long before anyone else. By working with exceptional children at the extremes of the ability range I also hoped to gain credibility with the teachers because I had experienced some of the difficulties they had with individuals.

The sessions with the children also served another important purpose. I achieved my objective of leaving the teachers to plan sequences of activities and to try these with their children on their own. On the other hand I was able to maintain informal contact with the schools, meeting the teachers to discuss my sessions with the children and listening to accounts of experiments made by individual teachers.

My aims when working on mathematics with the groups of children were similar to those when working with teachers during the two inputs. They should

(1) enjoy mathematics;
(2) become confident in their ability to learn mathematics through planned activities;
(3) discuss their findings with their peers and with their teacher;
(4) understand the mathematical concepts they use;
(5) see mathematics in action and realize why they need to memorize number facts and carry out calculations;
(6) appreciate that mathematics is concerned with patterns and the communication of these patterns in simple language.

At teacher-level I made my aims clear by planning the working sessions so that they mirrored the classroom organization I hoped the teachers would adopt. I provided a series of structured activities (focused on problems) which the teachers carried out in groups, discussing their ideas and comparing methods and solutions as they worked. I hoped that through working in this way the teachers would come to appreciate the value of activities and discussion, understand the mathematical concepts children needed to acquire together with the appropriate language patterns, and learn more mathematics.

(The support visits were planned to help teachers to adapt for their children the activities they had covered during the working sessions. I offered to work with any teacher in her classroom on any topic she chose. The most frequent request was for me to introduce activities on a specific topic with the children organized in groups. Gradually I shifted the responsibility for the planning to the teacher, acting as her helper until she was ready to take full responsibility for all the groups herself.)

At child-level, I planned sequences of activities for each group, although I was ready, at any time, to take up any suggestions made by the children to solve the problems which arose. I realized that for many children, as for their teachers, learning by means of activities was a new experience. The early activities therefore had to be simple and easily understood. Moreover, many children were unused to being asked to talk about what they were doing. I therefore had to question them more directly during the earlier sessions.

II. Overall structure

Three first and three middle schools and the associated high school were selected from each of two socially contrasting areas by the LEA advisers. The names given in this book were taken from the London telephone directory:

First schools	Middle schools
Frame	Melia
Fleet	Meakins
Foster	Missingham
Flanders	Movehall
Fowler	Makewell
Finlay	Measures

During the spring and summer terms of 1977 I visited each of the first schools (age range 5 to 8) and each of the middle schools (age range 8 to 12) five times at fortnightly intervals in the spring term and four times at weekly intervals in the summer term.

At each middle school four groups of children were nominated by the head and the teachers, one able group and one slow-learning one from the first two years and similar groups from the last two years. At each first school one able group and one slow-learning group were similarly nominated, each from the third and fourth years. The able groups contained six to nine children; the slow-learning groups four to eight. By spending a morning or afternoon on each visit to a first school and a full day on each visit to a middle school I hoped to have nearly an hour with each group. A visit of one day to each of the two high schools to which the middle schools contributed was arranged in order to maintain contact with them and to report progress. My immediate objectives were:

(1) to identify the particular learning problems of slow-learning children and to try to find ways of overcoming these;

(2) to provide able children with a variety of investigations and to note their reactions;

(3) to observe the attitude to mathematics of individual children and to notice whether there was any change by the end of the sessions;

(4) to try to discover the extent of each child's understanding of concepts and his knowledge of number facts, and to increase both;

(5) to meet the teachers of the children in each group after each session to discuss the activities covered and the children's responses, encouraging the teachers to continue the activities I had started.

III. External problems

There were two problems which were beyond the schools' control. All the schools had difficulty, with the numbers on roll at that time, in finding a room for an hour on end. Very few of the rooms in which I had to work were ideal from my point of view. I had expected that after the first few minutes the children would become accustomed to the surroundings and forget them. But discomforts (such as over-crowding, an uncomfortable temperature, lack of ventilation, chairs which were too high for the children's feet to reach the floor, noise from PE classes when working on the stage of a school hall) often led to behaviour problems.

The timing of the sessions also caused problems. Most of the project schools timetabled mathematics to take place in the morning. With my full programme of visits I had to work with some children in the afternoon. This meant that when children were working with me in the afternoon they had already had a mathematics lesson that day. Furthermore, they frequently had to miss lessons which they regarded as recreational, such as cooking, craft and physical education, in order to attend my sessions.

There was an additional problem in the fourth year of the middle school. All the children at this stage were apprehensive about the coming transfer to a high school, particularly during their final term at the middle school. The heads said that the behaviour of all these children deteriorated at that time. The able children were anxious about the choice of school (some of them were taking examinations for entry to independent schools); the slow-learning children were worried in case there would be no one who would understand their special problems. The transfer from first to middle schools did not seem to cause so much anxiety. Perhaps there was more contact between first and middle schools?

IV. Early planning of the sessions

In my planning I kept the following points in mind.

(1) Many children were unaccustomed to working in a group. Moreover, because of the two-year age span enforced by the limited time I had available, most of the children did not know all the others in their group. They were apprehensive and needed time to settle and get to know each other before they were prepared to make suggestions.

(2) Because the groups had my undivided attention, some of the children found it hard to maintain the continuous concentration required.

I planned sequences of activities to determine the extent of understanding each child had of mathematical concepts and the extent of number knowledge he had available for quick recall. In this way I ensured that the children made use of mathematics from the outset and talked about what they were doing. This was essential, not only to help me to assess individual children but also to show the children the reason for learning the number facts they did not know.

My over-riding aim was to help the children to become confident in their own ability to learn mathematics; even some of the able children had doubts about this. This help was given in various ways. First, I explained the purpose of the sessions to the children. They would be given mathematical activities to do, many of which would be new to them. Materials and equipment would be available but they might not need to use them. I wanted to find which of the activities they enjoyed and whether they found these too hard, too easy or just right. In this way they could help me with the experiment I was doing to try to find aspects of mathematics which particularly interested children.

Secondly, I adopted a positive approach at all times by giving the children encouragement for their achievements and never discouraging them; ensuring that they achieved a measure of success; providing attractive activities and games for them to enjoy; getting them to talk about what they had done; and making sure that they possessed an adequate and easily recallable number knowledge.

CHAPTER TWO

The activities used with slow learners in first schools and some of the children's responses

The activities provided for the first school slow learners (aged seven and eight years) revealed not only the extent of their understanding of mathematical concepts but also their knowledge of simple number facts. Whenever we attempted a new activity I made the children work in pairs, to encourage them to discuss what they were doing.

I. Content

A. Number patterns and operations on numbers

(1) I provided a set of jumbled number symbols 0 to 10, each on a separate card, for every child. The children were asked to name each symbol and then to arrange them in number order. Very few of them were unable to do this. A few subsequently had difficulty in matching the correct number of objects to the higher numerals.

(2) I introduced number patterns by giving each child a die. I asked them what they could find out about the number of dots on its opposite faces. This took a long time because none of the children recognized $\because$ or $\vdots$ at sight. We discussed how they could recognize these patterns without counting. At Frame, for example, some described $\because$ as: 'It's 4 at the corners and 1 in the middle', while others argued: 'It's 3 in a line and 1 each side'. Some described $\vdots$ as 2 and 2 and 2, and others said: 'It's 3 and 3'. They then made a written record of the sum of the pairs of numbers on opposite faces of the die, for example: 6 and 1 make 7.

(3) I provided other activities to give the children practice in recognizing the number of objects in sets without counting them. For example, I asked the children at Fowler to make models with 10 interlocking cubes and then to talk about the number of cubes in each part of the model. I ought to have foreseen the difficulties they would have. They frequently counted cubes twice. For example, they described the bridge (Figure 1):

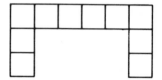

Figure 1

'I used 3 and 3 and 6 cubes to make this bridge. That makes 10 cubes.' So at Flanders I used pebbles instead. The children first described the patterns they made by scattering 10 pebbles on a sheet of paper. When, as I expected, they said that the '+' symbol meant 'Put together and say how many altogether', I let them shorten their written recording by using this symbol.

I then asked them if they could make a square using exactly 10 pebbles. They found that they could not do so, although they showed me that they knew what a square shape was, by pointing to squares in the room. They therefore made a rectangular frame.

'Can you make a square with 9 pebbles?' I asked. This took some time because they were trying to make a square frame instead of a square. When the square was made they described the number pattern: '3 and 3 and 3 make 9.'

B. Dice games

(1) I gave each pair of children a die. I asked them to throw the die in turn, taking and keeping pebbles at each throw to match the number they had thrown. After three throws each, I asked, 'Who has the higher total?' They did not know how to find out because they were unsure about matching one-to-one. At Foster, to help the children to appreciate the need for a baseline when making such comparisons, I asked the group to arrange themselves in height order.

This took time and many comparisons were made. The children said that it was easier to arrange children in height order than pebbles, but when I asked them to use interlocking cubes to match each dice score, they stood the resulting 'towers' of cubes on the table to compare them. I varied this activity by asking pairs of children to find out who was the first to score 20 or more when they were throwing a die in turn.

(2) Addition of dice scores. I gave each child two dice and asked them to add the scores and record the totals. Without exception, each child announced both scores and then counted the number of dots there were altogether, instead of adding the scores.

At Fleet, since Peter always knew which was the larger score, I suggested that he should cover that die with the other, count on the smaller score (to avoid counting all the dots over again) and record the total. I gave all the others practice in throwing two dice and showing me the larger score before they used Peter's method. Meanwhile, Peter was beginning to memorize the doubles and to add 1 at sight. I encouraged him, and the others, to record the scores at sight whenever they could.

Later on, I asked them to make a written record of the scores. This caused Jane, and others who were adept at finger counting, to count both scores on their fingers. 'To make sure', they said. The mere sight of an addition such as 6 + 3 made them use finger counting to find the answer. It was difficult to break them of this habit until they gained more confidence, especially when they had more than two numbers to add. Occasionally, I gave the children short written 'tests' on dice score addition, divided into sections such as the doubles, adding 1 (or 2), or reversals (4 + 3 = 3 + 4). The advantage of giving written tests was that many of the children succeeded with the addition of numbers up to 6 (36 facts in all), whereas they had often failed in the past when adding numbers from 1 to 10 (100 facts in all). Moreover, some children who were totally lacking in confidence when dealing orally with number facts were more successful when writing the answers to additions within the limited range. At a later stage I included subtractions within this range when the children had already subtracted the scores on a pair of dice.

When adding the scores on a pair of dice was an activity familiar to the children, I asked them to record the totals for 10 throws. 'Which total was thrown most often?' I asked. When I increased the number of throws to 20 this took them some time to work out. John, a third-year boy at Foster, decided to record his scores in order from now on, so I gave him squared paper to facilitate this type of recording. I asked the children to find the highest possible and the lowest possible scores. Most of them showed me the answer with the two dice. I then asked them if they could turn the dice over and get all the totals from 2 to 12. Once again, they used their dice to work this out. I gave each child a sheet of centimetre squared paper and explained that I was going to help them to record their totals in a quicker way. I asked them to write all the possible totals, 2 to 12, one in each square across the top row. 'How can you use this sheet to record each total?' I asked. 'If we throw 3 and 3 we write 6 in the 6 column', was the reply. I suggested that one child should throw the dice and announce the scores and the other should record the totals until I told them to exchange roles. They were to let me know which total 'won' (reached the bottom of the page first). One pair (at Foster) decided beforehand which total was going to win (5) and recorded this total whenever it seemed likely to lose, regardless of the scores! The children soon realised that when recording in this way they could tell at a glance which total occurred most often and least often. At Fleet, Dean and Susan, who were working together, organized a dice 'picture' to show in how many ways each total could be thrown.

(3) Dice subtraction. We then turned our attention to dice 'difference'. Most children did not understand the question: 'What is the difference between the two dice scores?', but they did understand 'How many more is the higher score?'. Most of them found the answer by covering on the die with the higher score the number of dots on the die with the lower score. Some children at Frame with a short span of concentration soon forgot that they were recording 'How many more?' and began to record totals again. By contrast, at the final session, the children at Foster recorded two additions and a subtraction for every pair of numbers they threw. They also prepared a dice subtraction sheet on squared paper for all the possible differences obtained when throwing a pair of dice.

C. Difference between two numbers

I reinforced the concept of the difference between two numbers by using interlocking cubes. At Fleet I asked each child to take ten cubes and to make two equal towers. To my surprise they all made five towers of two cubes each. When I repeated the request, emphasizing that I wanted two equal towers, they found the solution. I then asked them to make two unequal towers but there was no response, so I suggested that they should now make two towers, one taller than the other, and tell me how many more cubes there were in the taller one. Margaret had six cubes in one tower and four in the other. She said 'I have six more cubes in the taller tower'. The others agreed. It took some time, and practice at subsequent sessions, to establish the idea and the language pattern: 'I took six blue cubes and four red ones, so I have two more blue than red.' I thought the difficulty might lie in a misunderstanding of the concept of a baseline, so I asked them to arrange first two then three children in order of height. I next asked them to repeat this with one child standing on a chair. Immediately they said: 'It isn't fair; they must all stand on the floor.' We returned to this activity whenever we needed to find a difference, until the children used a baseline (often the edge of a table) whenever they met a difference problem.

I encouraged the children, as a group, to build all the different pairs of towers they could, using all ten cubes each time. I asked them to arrange the differences between the numbers of cubes in number order, and to tell me what they noticed about the differences. But they did not know odd and even numbers, so I could not continue this enquiry.

D. Odd and even numbers

At Fleet, after we had practised recognizing odd numbers by 'the odd man out', the one left when the others had taken a partner, I asked each child to take a sample of pebbles, to pair them and to show me whether any samples were odd. After preliminary practice, I suggested that they should each take ten samples, one at a time, and record whether each sample was odd or even. They counted the number of odd and even samples when they had finished pairing ten samples. I questioned them: 'Who has the same number of odd samples as even ones? Who has more even samples than odd? Who has fewer even than odd?' They did not know the word fewer but some guessed its meaning because this was the only possibility left.

E. Place value

The children showed in a variety of ways that they did not understand place value (digits reversed when writing scores, inability to realize, for example, that 10 + 6 is 16 etc.).

(1) At Fleet, Jane played a dice game, recording her score in pebbles on a place value sheet (Figure 2). She said: 'I have one ten and one pebble over'. When I asked 'How many is that altogether?' Jane counted all the pebbles and announced excitedly, 'I've got eleven pebbles'. I asked her to record: 11 = 10 + 1, and to play the game several times.

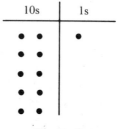

Figure 2

(2) At Finlay I asked each child to count out ten pebbles and to arrange these first in sets of 2, then in sets of 3, etc. They gave their results orally, for example: 'I've got three sets of 3 and 1 left.'

(3) I provided each child with a converted egg box to be used for two place value 'positions' (Figure 3). At the first session I told the children that we were going to count in fours today. I asked them to

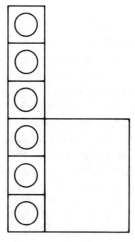

Figure 3: Converted egg box   **Figure 4: Place value sheet**

choose a 'nonsense' name for four because when we were counting in fours we must not use its name. At Frame the children chose 'pop' as the nonsense name for four. I explained that every time I rang my bell I wanted them to add one pebble to the unit compartment on the right of the egg box.

After each sound of my bell I asked for the score, encouraging the children to reply, for example, 'zero pops three ones'. I asked them what they would do when they had zero pops pop ones. They replied: 'Move the set of pop ones to an egg space.' I rang the bell. 'What is your score now?' I asked. 'One pop zero ones,' was the reply. I continued until the score was three pops three ones; every child had several turns at giving the score. I then repeated this activity using interlocking cubes, so that each set of pop cubes could be fastened together and moved to the left on a place value sheet (Figure 4). They called these new units popsticks. Again we stopped at three popsticks three ones. We repeated the activity, counting in fives (named 'bumps'); this time we stopped at four bumps four ones.

We had short practices at subsequent sessions, using different materials and either egg boxes or place value sheets. I asked the children to tell me what happened to each completed set. 'I moved them to an egg-space on the left,' was the reply. From time to time I asked the children to use the egg boxes to count a collection of between 20 and 30 pebbles in tens. When they did this correctly I asked them to record their scores: for example, $23 = 20 + 3$. (The children at Flanders always found it easier to record: $20 + 3 = 23$.)

(4) I reversed this activity, again using four as the first counting number. The children started with a score of three pops three ones; every time I struck a triangle they had to remove one unit from the total. When the score was three popsticks zero units I asked the children what they would do at the next 'strike'. 'Move one popstick, break it into units and remove one unit', they said. Unfortunately for the children at Fowler, I had not reinforced the addition activity sufficiently. After the first few subtractions some of the children began to remove one unit from a popstick without first moving the popstick to the right and breaking it into units. Some of them began to add instead. It took time to establish the subtraction routine in all the groups.

I varied the activity by giving the children different starting points (for example, two bumps three units) and asking them to change these bumps and units to units (or to change units into bumps and units).

We then concentrated first on counting a collection in tens and units and recording the answer, and secondly on estimating the number of pebbles in a collection and checking by counting the collection, patterning each ten so that I could check the recorded total at a glance. (My reason for giving much preliminary practice with counting numbers smaller than ten was that such activities took far less time. The children usually recognized the number of objects in a set without counting when this number was four or fewer, whereas when we counted a collection in sets of ten, they frequently had to count the number of units left over.)

(5) *Using multibase material.* After the gap of two months between the sessions of the spring and summer terms, I gave the children multibase material (base 4). I was determined to establish the language patterns of exchange. In all the groups I distributed the material so that each child had more than four pieces of each of the unit cubes, the rods and the squares. I observed what the children did. Without exception they built towers. When they had finished I asked them how they could find the tallest tower. They all replied, 'Measure'. But we had no rulers and the towers were too fragile to be moved. Peter, at Fleet, fetched a long paper strip and marked the height of each building on the strip. Jane piled up 'logs' but the logs toppled over, so she substituted cubes for logs (after first finding that the logs were the same height as the cubes). During this activity most of the children discovered the 'four' relationship between successive pieces of the material. I did not prompt this discovery.

(6) I explained the 'Build a square' game. At first I threw the die; the children matched each die score with units, changing these into logs whenever this was necessary. When the children were successful at this they played in pairs. At each throw each had to wait for his partner to tell him how many units to take and what exchanges to make. This was to give them practice in using the language of exchange and also as a check; if the 'teller' forgot to direct an exchange, his partner could claim an extra turn. At Flanders, Nick was always precise in his directions, finishing with the injunction: 'Put them on neatly'. Some children began to use short cuts. Nick told his partner, 'Take one log one unit', when the score was five. I asked him to explain why his statement was correct. Nick replied: 'Because one log is four units, so that makes five units altogether.'

I also taught the children 'Break a cube'. For this game they started with a big cube and subtracted the dice score at each throw. Once again, the thrower had to wait for instructions before he handled the material. The language pattern of exchange was established quickly this time and the children were evidently encouraged by their success. At Foster Matthew set an interesting problem one day: 'Could any of us make exactly a cube with the material you've given us?' All the children tried but none of the six was able to build a cube exactly; however, I was encouraged because a boy from one of the slow-learning groups had been interested and confident enough to volunteer a most worthwhile problem.

F. Miscellaneous activities

(1) *A stationery shop.* All the children found the shop attractive and made great efforts to read 'Today's price list', 'Bargains', etc. I had provided purses of money for the children to count. Although they were all able to recognize the coins, very few were able to say how much money each purse contained. They merely counted the number of coins and gave that as the total in pence. After two attempts I realized that helping the children to count money would take a disproportionate amount of time. (I explained the situation to the teachers and urged them to remedy this deficiency, using real money.) However, sorting and counting the stock and recording the totals were useful activities (particularly sorting the picture postcards). This activity showed me which children were most imaginative.

(2) *Picture puzzles.* Since some of the children had a very short attention span I made a variety of self-correcting picture puzzles. These were made from two identical boards divided into twelve sections. On one of the boards (kept whole) the sections contained the answers; on the other board (with a picture on the back) the corresponding sections contained the questions. This second board was cut into its sections. The child had to put each question card in the correct position on the uncut board (Figure 5). When the puzzle was completed, each card was turned over. If the picture was continuous, the children knew that their answers were probably correct. The puzzles included all the sets of number facts I was trying to help the children to memorize; for example, one more and one less than numbers up to 12; pairs of numbers adding to ten; subtraction of digits from ten; doubling and halving numbers up to 20 etc. When a child became restless, it was useful to suggest that he should work at a number puzzle.

10	3	5	16	Double 8	Halve 10	Halve 6	Double 5
		2	1	Halve 2	Double 1		

Picture on back; cut into sections

Figure 5: Picture puzzles

II. The progress of individual children

At each school I discussed my final records with the teachers and asked for their views. The composition of the slow-learning group at Finlay changed several times during the two terms, mainly because of absences. Here is my summary of the progress of the more permanent members of the group.

Vanessa has continued to work hard; she has shown slow but steady progress. She now knows the number facts associated with the addition and subtraction of the scores on two dice. She is beginning to extend this to numbers up to ten, but she still panics on occasions and gives a wild answer. She needs constant encouragement.

One of the children brought Darren to join the group when it was particularly depleted and he continued to attend. It was immediately evident that Darren had a greater understanding and knowledge of number than the others. During his time in the group he made spectacular progress. His teacher said that Darren came to me just as he was 'beginning to take off'. Perhaps because Darren was always interested in what we were doing and always made various suggestions for solving the problems I set, the others in the group made greater efforts and became more responsive. Darren was an asset throughout.

Jack has problems at home and is immature in his behaviour. It is always difficult to persuade him to try an unfamiliar activity. Once he has made up his mind to try a new problem, he usually becomes more confident. For example, he used multibase material confidently when he recognized the relationship between the pieces. He now knows the number of dots on each face of a die without counting, but there are no number facts which he can record. He can count the number of objects in a set which contains fewer than 20 objects but he cannot write the number. Ned is good with Jack, and often partners him in an activity so that he can encourage Jack to make a start. Ned is always quick to pick up an activity but his knowledge of number facts is sporadic, and he does not like making written records of results. Like Jack, he has to be coaxed and encouraged frequently.

The progress of some of the slow learners was uneven and, at times, indiscernible. Joan (at Frame) was lethargic and slow to respond to any activities, even when she had my full attention. She could count a set of objects up to five; except for • and •• she could not recognize the numbers of dots on the faces of a die without counting. Neither could she suggest a strategy for finding which of two sets had more objects.

At the third session she counted twelve objects with only one slip. At her request I therefore let her play 'adding the scores on two dice' and recording the totals. When I returned to observe Joan I found that if she threw two scores which she knew she could not add, she threw the dice again! I discussed this session with her teacher and suggested that Joan should have daily practice in making sets of objects to match the numerals 1 to 12, in random order, and then arranging the sets in number order. At the fifth session she was able to complete this activity successfully. I then asked her: 'How many is six more than five?' Joan counted out both sets, then pointed to the set of six saying, 'This has one too many'. She repeated this process for other numbers.

Joan was on holiday during the next session. When she returned to the seventh session she delighted me by her knowledge of one more and one less than numbers up to ten. She also volunteered: '3 and 1, and 1 and 3, are really the same sum.' But next time Joan was lethargic once more and seemed not to understand 'Build a cube', which she had mastered during the previous session. Her teacher came to tell me that she was depressed about Joan's apparent lack of progress. (The psychiatrist had said that there was nothing physical to account for Joan's reluctance to respond.)

By contrast, Jane's sudden progress (at Fleet) was maintained. When she returned after three weeks of illness she surprised me (and the head) by getting all the addition and subtraction bonds of ten correct. During the following (final) session she had no difficulty in converting a number of unit cubes 'to the fewest number of pieces'. She had come eagerly to the later sessions because she had gained confidence.

III. Findings from these sessions in first schools

None of the children was accustomed to being withdrawn for mathematics. Initially their overriding concern was to please. They tried to find out what I wanted them to do, instead of concentrating on a prolonged activity planned to help them to acquire a concept. They found the concentration required when working in a small group hard to maintain and switched off whenever they encountered any difficulty. The response of a few disturbed children remained unpredictable. The fact that they all disliked mathematics and did not expect to understand or to be able to do what I asked exacerbated their anxiety. The preliminary activities had to be simple so that only a short introduction would be necessary. The children needed frequent encouragement and appreciation for any achievement, however small. They had rarely enjoyed mathematics.

Many of the children in these slow-learning groups had difficulty in retaining number facts from session to session. (They probably required short daily practice, which I could not give them.) I was left wondering whether children in this age and ability range should be expected to memorize number facts systematically. Was it worth the great effort they would have to make?

It was clear that the activities I introduced did help these young slow learners to acquire the concepts of counting, of number order, of place value and of addition and subtraction. At the same time the children became familiar with the appropriate situations and the language patterns associated with them, which some of them were able to use for themselves. But these concepts are not the only ones which even young children need to acquire. Concepts underlying shapes, money and all the measures are equally important. They not only reinforce concepts in number but are attractive to children because they involve problems based on everyday things.

Throughout my regular visits to the project schools I received a great deal of help from the heads and the teachers, including those who visited to help with slow readers at some schools. Frequently they were able to supply information about the home background of individual children which helped me to understand behavioural problems. Moreover, individual teachers were relieved to find that I experienced difficulties similar to those they had with disturbed children, and appreciated theirs. A few of these children continued to present problems from time to time, throughout the two terms. Their performance showed great variation from session to session. Their teachers said that they sometimes required more attention than any one child within a class could be given.*

There was another way in which the heads gave me considerable support. I wondered whether the slow-learning children were putting all the effort they could into their work. I therefore asked the heads to come to some of the sessions. (All except three heads did so; there were extenuating circumstances for two of them.) The head's presence had an immediate effect on the attitude of some children to their work. I explained before the head arrived that I had asked her to come because I wanted to make sure that the members of the group were working as hard as they could. The head's presence also showed that she approved of my sessions with them. Some of the first school heads were dismayed to find that the slow learners performed at such a low level.

---

* Variability of performance was related specifically to disturbed children and is therefore not relevant to the summary on pp. 47–50.

CHAPTER THREE

The activities used with slow learners (aged 8 to 10 years) in the middle schools and some of the children's responses

Each of the groups contained at least two disturbed children who needed constant attention in the earlier sessions if they were to cooperate in any activity. For example, at Movehall, Pauline was fearful of undertaking any activity on her own. She rarely listened to my introduction to a problem and noisily interrupted to protest that she did not understand. My response, since she was fascinated by my calculator, was to set her a calculation until I could help her to come to terms with the current activity. (She was always the first to volunteer to carry or distribute material.)

Matthew, in the same group, had a hearing defect. It was therefore difficult to know whether he had heard an explanation or not; he seldom started an activity at the same time as others in the group. I usually had to assume that he had not heard. (Eventually he went to a special school.) Unless I worked with him on his own he achieved very little. Florence was quiet but she too had to be prodded at frequent intervals. David and Alice usually worked well but both could be distracted by the others. This was a small group but not an easy one to manage.

I. General points

(1) There was a wider range of ability among the children in these groups than among those at the first schools. During the two terms of my work with these children three of them were promoted to a higher mathematics set. Although all the children gained an understanding of mathematical concepts such as division, multiplication and subtraction, a few continued to find the memorization of number facts extremely difficult.

(2) There were far more absences, especially at Measures, than at the first schools. New children were often added to the groups when there were persistent absences but this usually upset the group temporarily.

(3) There were some behaviour problems, particularly during the first two sessions.

II. Content

A. Number patterns and number facts

Although the children had not been given any of the activities before, most of them had little difficulty in understanding what I asked them to do. I covered a range of activities in the first session to find out how much the children understood and which number facts they had memorized. The range of activities is shown by my notes of the first session at Makewell, which follow. (There were six boys in this group, three from each year.)

Orally this group did well. They were able to estimate the number of pebbles in a collection, to arrange their 'count' in tens and units, and, with one exception, to say how near each count was to their estimate. When I asked them to tell me pairs of numbers whose sum was ten, they offered some of these and recorded their results. We then began to add ten to numbers fewer than ten. At first they were clearly counting on in ones, but by the time we had finished, even the slowest pair could state the sum at once. To reinforce and extend this activity we added and subtracted ten to and from numbers fewer than 100. Two first years became very quick at this and soon became bored. Yet when I asked Neil to add the single column of numbers collected from throwing a die, he said, 'I don't know how to do addition'. Ultimately, he found the total by counting on his fingers.

The children seemed so competent orally that I gave them an odds and evens activity.* I asked them to take ten samples of pebbles, one at a time, and to record whether each sample was odd or even. They then recorded the total number of evens and odds they had in their samples and gave their results to Geoffrey to find the grand total. He, too, counted on his fingers to obtain this total. We then added the

---

* Not all the children could distinguish odd from even numbers. At Melia the other children explained to Liz: 'You find even numbers by putting the collection in twos. If there is one over it [the number of objects in the collection] is odd.'

results aloud. When I asked them to add 10 and 7 they all counted on their fingers. I reminded them that ten minutes previously they had told me the answers without any finger counting. To reinforce quick addition of ten we then used a number line. When the answers were between 100 and 110, all except two older boys recorded the number as, for example, 1003.

Finally, we discussed our totals from the odds and evens activity. There had been 36 evens and 34 odds. They checked that the total 70 was correct because seven of us had each taken ten samples. I asked them what the scores for evens and odds would be if these had been equal. It took some time for them to decide that this must be 35. I then asked them which result was nearer to 35, 34 or 36. Again, they took a long time to answer this question. I think it was the unfamiliarity of the question which puzzled them. Not all the groups covered so much ground during the first session.

At Melia, Charles and Liz had already worked on the odds and evens activity with their teacher. During their experience of this with me they showed great confidence and settled immediately to work. Indeed Liz, who had burst into tears at my initial interview with her, gradually increased in confidence throughout the sessions. It was a great help that her teacher also gave her encouragement.

The children in all the groups had difficulty in transferring their individual results to my group table, which was always identical with the tables I helped individuals to prepare. I realized that several of the children were slow readers but I always made sure that they could read the words ('odds' and 'evens' in this activity) before they entered their results. I wondered whether they were apprehensive because they knew that they would be called upon to find the totals?

B. Dice games

The children in these groups played the dice games more confidently than those at the first schools. All could recognize the number of dots on each face of a die without counting. They were therefore quick to discover the dice pattern – the sum of the numbers on opposite faces of a die (seven). At Meakins I then asked the children to find the sum of the numbers 1 to 6. They did not associate this sum with the sum of the numbers on the opposite faces on a die. When they obtained 21 by counting the set one to six, I pressed them to use their discovery about the opposing faces of a die. Jack said: 'Find three sevens. Two sevens are 14; one more makes 21.' (He added by counting on from 14.)

We then progressed to adding the scores on two dice. They began by counting the dots on both dice but they were all able to tell me which was the larger of two scores. It was therefore an easy step to persuade them always to add on the smaller score, until they began to memorize the combinations of the pairs of numbers. For this and similar activities I organized the children to work in pairs, one throwing, the other recording, in turns. But Charles at Melia insisted on recording every result himself and in full: for example, 2 + 6 = 8. He was therefore always slower than his partner and unable to work with her. We soon progressed to recording the results in order, on squared paper*. Recording in this way helped the children to analyse their results. It was easy to find the total which occurred most frequently. I then asked each child at Melia to make an addition table for the numbers one to six (Table 1). They made heavy weather of this. Charles saw the pattern and raced through. When I asked him to record how many times each total occurred, he discovered a pattern for the numbers in the lower half of the table. Working from the pattern he recorded: 2 occurs once, 3 occurs twice, 4 occurs 3 times, 5 occurs 4 times, 6 occurs 5 times, 7 occurs 6 times [correct]. He then continued: 8 occurs 7 times, 9 occurs 8 times, etc. This experience shook his confidence in pattern for a time! He would of course have been right if he had been able to extend the table beyond the numbers obtainable from his dice. I asked them what was the same about the totals in the table and about finding the totals by throwing two dice, but no one could say.

Table 1: Addition of pairs of numbers from the set 1 to 6

6	7	8	9	10	11	12
5	6	7	8	9	10	11
4	5	6	7	8	9	10
3	4	5	6	7	8	9
2	3	4	5	6	7	8
1	2	3	4	5	6	7
+	1	2	3	4	5	6

---

* Desmond at Missingham declared that all his totals occurred 28 times. When I enquired about his method he said, 'When a total gets behind I wait for it to turn up before recording any other total'.

Surprisingly, all the children enjoyed finding and recording the differences between the scores on two dice more than they enjoyed any other activity (Table 2). Pauline, at Movehall, for the first time finished recording and analysing twenty results before any one else in the group. Was this because the numbers involved were small? When we discussed the possible differences which we could get when throwing a pair of dice, Rodney (at Missingham) said '6 must be the largest'. But Norman disagreed: 'You can't have a difference of 6 because you don't have 7 on a die.'

Table 2: Differences ($\sim$) between pairs of numbers 1 to 6.

6	5	4	3	2	1	0
5	4	3	2	1	0	1
4	3	2	1	0	1	2
3	2	1	0	1	2	3
2	1	0	1	2	3	4
1	0	1	2	3	4	5
$\sim$	1	2	3	4	5	6

C. Place value

In all the groups most of the children could interpret numbers such as 53 as 50 + 3 but they had had little experience of numbers greater than 100. Moreover, none had grasped the significance of the addition and subtraction of ten to any two-digit number. At least one child in every group was confused about place value; for example, Ronald at Melia wrote 17 for 70, 18 for 80, etc; Rodney at Missingham frequently reversed the digits.

Although most children understood the significance of position in determining the value of a digit, they found it difficult to rewrite 50 + 3 as 40 + 13. Since this was a useful strategy in subtraction I gave the children experience in rewriting two-digit numbers by providing interlocking cubes to represent the numbers. As each ten-stick was moved to the units column it was broken into units and a record was made.

(1) *Dice games*. I used various games to ensure that the children had different experiences of applying the concept of place value. For example, the children played place value games using dice of different sizes. In the simpler version where the score on the larger die

represented the number of tens, they threw two dice six times in all. At each throw the children recorded their scores in tens and units; they then arranged the scores in number order from smallest to largest. In the harder game three dice of different sizes were thrown at a time, the largest die representing 'hundreds' and the smallest 'units'. After my explanation Jack at Meakins said: 'I don't get it. Tell me what to do.' Yet once Jack began the game he very soon progressed to the three-dice version. I asked him: 'How do you know which is smaller, 641 or 614?' Jack replied: 'The hundreds are the same but one number has four tens and one unit, the other has one ten and four units. 614 is smaller.' I then suggested that they could find their total score, earning one point for every ten (or 100). This gave them another opportunity for adding a single column of figures; I found that I had to remind them to try not to use their fingers!

(2) *Number cards.* In another useful game the children played in pairs with a pack of well shuffled cards (two sets labelled 1 to 9), placed face down. Each child prepared a place value sheet (Figure 2, p. 12) on which to put two cards, one in each column. The child with the higher two-digit number was the winner. Each child in turn took a card and decided in which column to put it. The second card had to be placed in the empty column. Each child announced his score. The winner gained an extra point if he could say by how many he had won (using a number line if necessary). Later on, the game was changed to make the child with the lower number the winner. The games helped me to assess each child's understanding of place value and the extent to which he was able to develop strategies.

(For the children who were confused about place value I introduced 'Build a cube' and 'Break a cube' using multibase four and a single die. It was encouraging for Ronald at Melia when he was able to tell me: 'I changed four rods for a square and then four squares for a cube.')

(3) *Number lines.* Number lines were powerful tools for developing the concept of place value.

(a) Every child made his own number line from a metre strip of centimetre-squared paper, two centimetres wide. I asked the children to label the beginning 0 (zero) and the end, 100. When I explained that the number lines could also be used for measuring lengths, the children decided to number the 'measure' on the lines, and not in the spaces, 'because you would not know which was which', they said. I suggested that they should label the half-way mark first. It was some time before they all decided that the easiest way to find the middle of the number line was to fold the strip. Ronald at Melia merely guessed, and adjusted the ends only when I asked him how he could check that his guess was right. Before the children labelled the tens I gave them oral practice in multiplying single digits by ten, counting in tens, and saying how many tens there were in various multiples of ten. They labelled each interval of ten in one colour, and the inter-mediate intervals of five in another colour.

(b) The boys in the group at Meakins were reluctant to make a number line because they were missing football (and had already had a mathematics lesson that day). I asked them to use their number lines to measure and record, in a book about themselves, their personal statistics (perimeters of head, face, neck, etc.). For once, they worked most unwillingly. Only the girls completed the activity of recording how much shorter than a metre each measure was.

(c) The number lines were also used with a ten-strip for quick addi-tion and subtraction of ten to numbers within the range. This practice had a good effect on Pauline (at Movehall). For the first time she completed a picture puzzle for the addition and subtrac-tion of ten in record time.

(d) David (at Movehall) used his number line for doubling and halv-ing numbers, and recorded the results. The children in every group had already used their number lines to double their neck measure and compare this with their waist measure, and also to halve their waist measure and compare this with their neck measure.

(e) Later on, number lines were used to help the children to carry out calculations using the four operations.

D. The four operations

My first task was to find the extent of each child's understanding of each of the four operations. They understood addition. From time to time I asked the children to make and describe 'scatter patterns' of sets of pebbles. But it took time to get them to suggest that addition was 'putting sets of objects together and counting to find how many there were altogether'. When the children at Meakins made this state-

M*1: THE FOUR OPERATIONS
A summary of the basic situations and the appropriate language patterns
1. Addition
Patterning of a specific number of objects, for example, ten pebbles.

Oral description of the sets, gradually refined. The teacher introduces

(i) the addition symbol + to be understood as 'putting sets together and saying how many there are altogether'. Finding the total.

(ii) The symbol = for 'is equal to', meaning 'is equivalent to' (rather than 'is identical with').

2. Subtraction
Two different starting situations, three language patterns.

(i) One set; 'taking away' situation. For example, 'I had seven toy cars but I lost two. How many are left?' $7 - 2 = 5$.

'I had nine shells; I gave three to Marilyn. How many have I now?' $9 - 3 = 6$.

(ii) Comparison of two sets. (a) For example, 'I took ten red and three blue cubes. How many more (fewer) are there in the larger (smaller) set?' $10 - 3 = 7$.

Using measures: 'How much more (less) does the mug hold than the cup?'

(b) 'What is the difference in number between the scores five and two on two dice?' $5 - 2 = 3$, or 'What is the difference in capacity (length, etc.) between the two containers?'

3. Division
Two different starting situations; three language patterns.

(i) 'Share 12 shells among three children. How many does each have?' (Divide 12 into three equal sets.) Later on, 'Find one third of 12 shells'. $12 \div 3 = 4$.

(ii) 'How many children can have three shells each?' This is solved by each child in turn taking three shells until there are none left. (12 divided into sets of 3: successive subtraction of 3).

4. Multiplication
Two different situations; two language patterns.

(i) 'Four sets of 3 pebbles. How many altogether?' (Addition of equal sets.) $3 \times 4 = 12$. In mathematics the number in the set is usually recorded first.

(ii) Magnification; find a number three times as many as 5. $5 \times 3 = 15$.

Or, cut a length of ribbon four times as long as eight centimetres.

---

* 'M' indicates an insertion of special mathematical significance, of which there are several in the text altogether.

ment, they showed me the addition symbol and subsequently used this symbol to describe the scatter patterns they made.

All the children had already found how near their estimate of the number of pebbles in a collection was to the actual number. This showed me that they understood the comparison aspect of subtraction. This aspect was reinforced when they found the differences between the scores on a pair of dice. I therefore decided that I would try to help those children with a sufficient knowledge of subtraction facts to make a written record of subtraction situations. I was influenced in my decision by the fact that most of the children were expected by their teachers to do written addition and subtraction of two-digit numbers (and sometimes of three-digit numbers!). There were three reasons why these children were unable to do such calculations. They did not understand the method they had been shown; they were not familiar with the situations which require the operation of subtraction for their solution; they had not memorized sufficient number facts.

We began by recording 'shopkeeper's addition'. As before, I provided a stationery shop, with purses containing money, and asked each child to buy one article costing less than 50 pence and to check the change the shopkeeper gave. I realized that they would find recording difficult, so I suggested that the child receiving change should record this as he received it. The other child would record his running totals. For example, at Melia Ronald spent 17 pence.
He recorded: Shopkeeper Liz recorded:

Change in pence	Totals in pence
	17
3	
	20
20	
	40
10	
—	50
33	

When the children were familiar with the process of giving change, I gave them practice in using the number line so that we were not restricted to coin values. At Measures I began asking the group: find 18 on the number line. Which is the next ten? How far away is 18? We then began to record some simple subtractions, using the number line. For example, at Measures the children found and recorded 32 − 19. They wrote, recording the running totals:

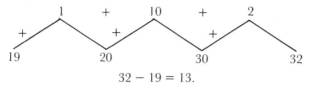

$$32 - 19 = 13.$$

When the children were able to record the subtraction without using a number line, they used the number line to check their result.

Ellen, at Measures, returned after an absence of three weeks. She found shopkeeper's addition difficult. I asked her how she could rewrite 73 in tens and units. She wrote 73 = 70 + 3. 'What would you have to add to 13 to make 73?', I asked, '60', she replied. I suggested that she should rewrite 73 so that she could subtract 37 from it. Ellen then recorded:

$$73 = 70 + 3$$
$$= 60 + 13$$

$$
\begin{array}{r}
60 + 13 \\
\text{subtract } 30 + 7 \\
\hline
30 + 6 \ = 36.
\end{array}
$$

73 − 37

Ellen was excited by this method and worked several subtractions in this way. When I introduced other children in the group to the method, Ellen was always ready to lend a helping hand. Not many children were willing to practise a second method when they had been successful with one.

I tried to help every group to understand the relation between multiplication and addition. I gave each child at Missingham 12 pebbles and asked them to arrange these in sets of 4. They arranged the pebbles in a rectangle and volunteered: 'If you look at the pattern in another way it shows four sets of 3, which make 12.' When I asked the children to write each of these statements using addition symbols they wrote: 4 + 4 + 4 = 12 and also 3 + 3 + 3 + 3 = 12. But it was some time before I could persuade them that they could also write the statements using the multiplication symbol. They needed to practise all four statements in different situations.

$$4 + 4 + 4 = 12, \quad 4 \times 3 = 12, \quad 3 + 3 + 3 + 3 = 12, \quad 3 \times 4 = 12$$

I then began to encourage them to memorize the table of twos. They built the table using identical squares, recording the multiplication facts as they progressed (Figure 6).

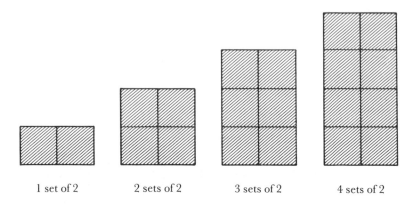

| 1 set of 2 | 2 sets of 2 | 3 sets of 2 | 4 sets of 2 |

Figure 6

We also built up the multiplication tables as far as multiplication of ten by numbers fewer than ten. (I emphasized that once they knew the table of multiplication by two, they could work out the other multiplication tables.)

I then asked the children to give me one example from everyday life when they used multiplication. There was no response. 'Don't you ever go shopping?', I asked. At last Ellen said that she had bought three packets of biscuits on Saturday, costing 21 pence each. 'How could you work this out?' I asked. Ellen wrote:

$$21p$$
$$21p$$
$$21p$$

and added to get the answer. I asked them how else they could find the answer. There was no response, so I asked them to learn the multiplication table of threes. At the next session I showed them how to record 21×3 as $20 + 1$

$$\underline{\times 3}$$

$$60 + 3 = 63$$

We did not have time to develop this further, but when I asked the children why they thought they were asked to learn multiplication tables Norman said, 'Multiplication is a quick way of adding'. I asked the teachers to follow this up.

The group at Makewell had already practised doubling numbers by using a number line but they had not found this operation easy. I now provided ten-sticks and units for doubling (and later on trebling, etc.). For example: 37 × 2. They put out material as in Figure 7.

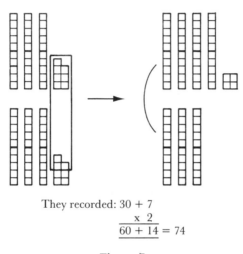

They recorded: 30 + 7
               x 2
            60 + 14 = 74

Figure 7

To develop the concept of multiplication further, in other groups I provided identical unit squares and asked the children to make some larger squares. All the children in the group at Makewell told me that a square has all its sides the same, but they all made rectangles instead of squares. Each had taken a handful of identical squares and they found it difficult to change the rectangle to a square. Eventually they arranged their squares in size order and recorded the sequence. I encouraged the children to memorize the square numbers. At the next session Alan said he wanted to make the square of 13, but he ran out of unit squares after three rows. 'But it doesn't matter', he said, 'because I know that 10 thirteens are 130. So 13 thirteens must be 169'. This achievement astonished me; it marked the beginning of spectacular progress on Alan's part and his eventual promotion to a higher mathematics set.

The children had already encountered one aspect of division in the odds and evens activity in which they paired a collection of pebbles to find out whether there was an odd one over. Perhaps this was why most of the children, including all those at Melia, put the pebbles in sets of 4 when I asked them to divide a set of 12 pebbles by 4. They all declared that they were 'sharing by four'. So I rephrased the question: 'Have I enough for everyone to have four pebbles each? How can we find out?' 'Let's each take four and see', they suggested. As each child took four I asked him to tell me what he had done and to record this. The first child, Ronald, said, 'I've taken my four', and the children recorded: $12 - 4$. The final record was: $12 - 4 - 4 - 4 = 0$. 'How many are left?' I asked; 'None', was the reply. 'Three children had four each', they finished.

I asked the group to divide 16 pebbles by two. This time only Liz put the collection into sets of 2; the others made two sets (of 8). I explained that both arrangements were correct. We recorded:

$$16 \div 2 = 8.$$ There are 8 sets of 2 or 2 sets of 8.

E. Memorization of number facts

Nearly all the slow learners found the memorization of number facts and their retention over an extended period extremely difficult, however willing they were to learn. Most of them worked hard to learn the number facts to be included in the next test but forgot them before the next session, one or two weeks later. Before Ellen, at Measures, was absent for three weeks, she had learned all the essential addition and subtraction facts. When she returned, at the beginning of the session she appeared to have forgotten all she had learned. She was clearly depressed so I gave her an activity she had missed. But by the end of the session she said: 'You can give me a test now. I remember all the facts I'd forgotten.' This made me realize that it is important not to pressurize children when they return to school after a break. They need time before they can extract facts from their long-term memory.

The children might well have found it easier to memorize and retain number facts if I could have followed the work up at frequent intervals.

III. The progress of individual children

Judging from my notes, I felt that every child in these groups made progress in understanding the concepts of addition, subtraction, multiplication and division. A few children made very noticeable progress. Alan, a second year at Makewell, was one of three children from the slowest mathematics set who were subsequently promoted by the mathematics coordinator. At first he appeared to be easily led by a younger boy. When I found out that the younger boy was his cousin, Alan's attitude to his work with me seemed to change. At the second session I had asked the children in this group to take ten samples of pebbles and to divide each by three. They were to record whether each sample was a multiple of three or not. Alan finished first. When all the results were collected I asked all the children to find the group's totals of multiples of three and non-multiples, urging them to look for pairs of numbers whose sum they knew, to prevent them from counting on their fingers. Only Alan managed this.

At the third session Alan arrived first and settled immediately to throwing two dice repeatedly and recording each total. He completed more examples than anyone else in the group.

At the fourth session the children labelled metre strips to be used as number lines and also for measuring their personal statistics. When they had recorded this information, I asked them to arrange all the measures in order and to find the difference between each pair. But they lost interest. Alan, once more, seemed to be easily led.

At the fifth session Alan said that he now knew all his multiplication tables, but I did not have time to test him. I asked the group to use their number lines to halve and double several numbers fewer than 100. Alan seemed to have particular difficulty and made several slips. He was absent on a school trip for the next session.

At the seventh session we used number lines to subtract numbers, and recorded the results, using 'shopkeeper's addition'. Alan was successful at the calculations and the recording. All the others found the recording difficult. I also tested Alan orally on the multiplication table of six. He had all the jumbled facts correct in record time.

During the eighth session the group built squares, using identical unit squares. While the others in the group were trying to make a complete sequence Alan started with one unit in the middle and made his own sequence. He discovered the pattern and made a written record.

In the final session we concentrated on squares once more. Alan had said that he knew all the multiplication facts as far as 15 × 15. He was able to demonstrate this when he was trying to make a square 13 units by 13. I asked him who had been giving him so much help and encouragement at home. He replied: 'My father has helped me ever since I was born.' I was so impressed by the effort Alan had made that I suggested to the coordinator that he deserved consideration for promotion. (He had already been promoted for reading.) After the coordinator had discussed this with his teacher, Alan received his well-deserved promotion.

Alan's progress demonstrates the importance of securing parents' cooperation in children's learning, especially when the children are having difficulties. Cooperation will be more effective if the parents are fully informed, at first hand, about the school's aims and methods.

IV. Findings from these sessions

1. Many children were so lacking in confidence that they always expected to be wrong. Whenever they succeeded at any activity or used a language pattern correctly, I seized the opportunity to give them the encouragement they always needed.

Some over-anxious children found it difficult to listen to my initial explanation of any problem I wanted them to tackle. Moreover, they switched off if they did not understand; I had to keep this hazard constantly in mind.

2. I thought it important for these children to be helped to memorize, systematically, some essential number facts, since this would help them in the work their teachers expected them to do. I found that short written tests on one particular set of number facts (such as the doubles of numbers one to ten) were often within their capabilities and made them settle more quickly. Furthermore, the children in all these groups enjoyed the picture number puzzles, which gave them the opportunity for further practice. However, if I was working with the remainder of the group it was not always easy to check that an individual child was using efficient methods of recall.

3. As with the first school groups, as soon as these children were asked to find the total of four or more single-digit scores, they counted on their fingers. They were usually quick at this from frequent practice! It took time to help them to memorize sets of number facts and to become sufficiently confident to apply this knowledge.

4. With this age group I was able to include problem situations (and the appropriate language patterns) which required the use of one or other of all four operations for their solution. With some groups I introduced written subtraction, using the shopkeeper's addition method.

I was surprised to find that none of these children could suggest problem situations which could be solved by multiplication. Even after I had asked them to give me an example from shopping, they solved the example by addition!

CHAPTER FOUR

Activities used with slow learners (aged 10 to 12 years) and some of their responses

I. General points

1. In all the schools except one there were one or more children who were prone to disturb the others from time to time, despite a gradual overall improvement in attitude.

2. In general the activities provided did not differ greatly from those used with the younger children, but they were covered in more depth.

3. With few exceptions, these older children started with a wider and more secure knowledge of number facts (particularly in addition and subtraction) than their younger counterparts.

4. The extent of the work covered in any session usually depended on the children's attitude to mathematics. For example, Richard, at Meakins, volunteered from the outset that he disliked mathematics. Diana did her best to avoid attending the sessions, on a variety of pretexts. At the third session she declared, 'I hate maths'. After this outburst she seemed to come willingly and made progress. Dorothy, who joined the group later on, said: 'I like maths but I can't do it.' Most of the children said that they liked mathematics only when they were successful.

II. Content of the sessions

A. Initial work with number

The contrast in the amount of ground covered by the different groups was evident from the first session, as my notes for Melia and Makewell illustrate. At Melia there were two third years and three fourth years.

This was a very willing group and they worked hard for nearly an hour. They usually gave thoughtful answers and had good ideas. They knew the bonds of ten and after a little practice answered without hesitation. They were able to add and subtract ten from numbers fewer than 100. When I asked for a quick way of adding nine, Margaret answered, 'Add ten and take off one'. I gave them practice in adding nine until they were quick and accurate. When I began to ask them to add near doubles (for example, seven and eight) Margaret said, 'I added seven and seven and then one more'. Ella doubled eight and 'took one away'. I then asked each to write a number fewer than nine and to add nine continuously (using Margaret's method) until they 'topped' 100. Then they added the digits and we discussed the surprising results. They were evidently enjoying what they did. When we played the odds and evens sampling game, they were able to find the average score (30) of 26 evens and 34 odds. Mick said: 'The scores are eight different; they are the same number away from the average.' The achievement of this group was particularly encouraging because neither of the class teachers was prepared to cooperate with me, despite the appreciation I expressed of the children's knowledge.

At Makewell there were three children from each of the third and fourth years. They, too, were a hardworking group. All of these children were able to arrange a collection of pebbles in tens and units and to compare the total with the initial estimate they had made. But when I asked them how far the collection they had taken was from 100 they found this difficult, even when I provided them with number lines. (Irene was the weakest. She knew neither the bonds of ten, nor the sequence 10, 20, 30, ...) When I gave them the odds and evens sampling activity, they recorded the results sensibly but took some time to realize that the total number of samples we had taken was 70. When I asked them what the number of odds and evens would be if these were equal I had no response at all. I therefore began to ask them to halve numbers, beginning with multiples of ten. When finally they found that half 70 was 35, I asked which of the scores (34 even, 36 odd) was nearer to 35. Again it was some time before David said: '34 is one below 35 and 36 is one above.'

B. Number facts

Once the children had gained confidence I encouraged them to talk about their methods of carrying out simple mental calculations, in particular how they would obtain a fact they did not know from others they could recall easily. Moreover, their knowledge of number facts gradually increased as we concentrated on a few related facts at each session. Whenever practicable I provided ten-sticks and units and number lines, so that the children could discover a particular set of facts before they began to memorize them. During the following session I 'tested' their knowledge orally, or by written answers, or by asking them to complete the appropriate number puzzle. Gradually they came to realize that the number facts they needed to learn were interrelated, that it was useful to be able to recall them quickly and that such memorization was not beyond them. Furthermore, the comparison of methods, which I always encouraged, helped to show them that there were often several solutions to a problem and that I set a value on all of them.

Some of the other children had other ways of thinking about numbers and their relationships.

(1) The group at Melia were adding pairs of numbers such as eight and six. Mick said: 'I took one from the eight and put it on the six to make seven and seven, that's 14.' Ella commented: 'Since we talked about adding numbers like nine and seven I've become much quicker. [She had!] To add nine and seven I said two sevens are 14 and two more make 16.' Hazel said: 'I added nine and seven by adding ten and subtracting one'.

(2) Richard at Meakins said: 'I know that six and five make 11 because if it had been one more that would have been two sixes – and that's 12.'

(3) Robert, at Missingham, announced one day, 'I know the nine times table now'. I asked him what six nines were but he replied: 'I only know that one if I say the table right through.' When I asked him five nines he answered quickly, '45, because ten nines are 90. So six nines must be 54. I added ten to 45 and then took one away.'

(4) The children at Measures were having difficulty with the table of threes. I asked them to build the tables on squared paper, beginning with the tables of one and two. I then asked them how they could find the table of threes from the tables of one and two. 'Add one and two', they answered at once. When I asked them how they could find the table of fours Darren said, 'Double the twos'; Sheila suggested, 'Add the threes and ones'. The children were evidently encouraged by this activity because Darren asked: 'Why is it that I always do better with you than I do in class?'

(5) One day Robert at Missingham asked what a square number was. So I asked the group to make a sequence of squares, using unit squares. Allen, who had made an eight by eight square, remarked that square numbers must be the number of small squares they had used to make each square. They each began to say how many units they had used. When they began to count the number of units Allen had used, I asked them if they could find the total without counting. Allen said: 'I know five eights are 40, so six eights are 48; two eights are 16, that makes 64.' Sandra said: 'I took two eights from ten eights (80).'

C. Dice and other games and activities

All the children had difficulty when adding six or more single digits. Initially they all counted in ones or used their fingers. Dice games were useful in providing natural opportunities for such addition. For example, the children (in pairs) recorded the sum of the scores on two dice. At first the scores were recorded successively but subsequently the children prepared a table on squared paper for recording the totals (Table 3). From this table they found out how often each total occurred. Several pairs found that seven occurred most frequently. 'In how many ways can you throw a total of seven with two dice?' I asked. They worked this out using pairs of dice, and then continued to find all the results for other possible totals. Finally I asked them to make an addition table for pairs of numbers (Table 1, p. 23) from one to six, and to find the frequencies of the totals in this table. They did not find any difficulty until I asked them what was the same about this addition table and their tables of dice scores. It was some time before anyone suggested that the pairs of numbers added in each example were taken from the numbers one, two, three, four, five, six. This and other dice games gave the children frequent practice in addition. They were given further practice: first in finding the difference between the scores on a pair of dice; then in adding these differences to find their total score.

Table 3: Sum of the scores on two dice

2	3	4	5	6	7	8	9	10	11	12
			✓		✓	✓				
					✓					

The children at Melia also recorded the results they obtained from multiplying the scores on a pair of dice. When they analysed their results I asked them which products they had failed to get. Ella said: 'Seven. We can't get seven because seven is not on the dice.' They had 19 results of 12. 'Why did we get so many 12s?' I asked. This made them use pairs of dice to find the different ways in which pairs of numbers one to six could be multiplied to obtain a product of 12.

Few children had difficulty in learning the 'hundreds, tens and units' activity in which dice of three sizes were used. (The largest showed the number of hundreds and the smallest the number of units.) At each throw each child recorded the score as a three-digit number. After six throws the children arranged the numbers in order of size; they had no difficulty in explaining the order in which they had arranged the numbers. Since one point was scored for each 100 when the children made their throws, this gave them further practice in adding single-digit numbers to find their total scores.

The 'odds and evens' sampling activity provided further opportunities for quick addition of scores. This activity was developed further in some schools. For example, at Meakins the children found that the number pattern of the units digit of all even numbers was two, four, six, eight, zero. At Missingham the children were already familiar with odds and evens sampling. I therefore asked them to take ten samples each, divide each into sets of four and record the remainders each time. They then found the total number of samples for each remainder: zero, one, two and three, and arranged these in order. There were 70 samples in all. When I asked them what the totals for each remainder would have been if they had all been the same, there was no response until I suggested guessing. They guessed ten first but that gave a grand total of 40. Subsequent guesses were 15 and finally 17, which they agreed was nearest (grand total 68). When they looked at the results they said that zero remainder occurred 17 times, but remainder three occurred six times only. (No conclusions could be drawn from so few samples.)

D. The four operations (see M1|p.27)

During the initial sessions I had asked the children to tell me which aspects of mathematics they found difficult. At Missingham Sandra said: 'I'm happy about fractions because we've been doing them recently. But I cannot do division.' Tracy added, 'And I can't do "times" either'. The others agreed. During the same session Tracy was scornful when Sandra could not add ten to 23 immediately. But Robert reproached Tracy saying, 'We all have problems with mathematics'.

We spent a good proportion of the time on the four operations. I was determined to ensure that the children would understand situations which require the use of one or other of the four operations for their solutions, and that they would use the correct language patterns. Only then could we review the methods of calculation the children were being taught. It was easy to check both their understanding of addition and their knowledge of addition facts during the written scoring for the games we played. There was only one girl (Irene at Makewell) who had difficulty with two-digit addition; hitherto she had always begun addition with the left-hand column. It took some time to cure her of this. Informal subtraction situations also developed from many different activities such as estimating and checking the number of objects in a collection, recording the differences of the scores on two dice, finding which personal measure was nearest to half a metre. I was able to assess whether the children could solve these subtraction problems, and whether they understood and could use the correct language patterns, and knew the subtraction facts (more difficult than the addition facts). It was important, too, to check that they could record, using symbols, the results obtained from the situations. To help them to memorize the subtraction facts I gave the children practice in completing subtraction trios (for example, two, five, is completed by three since $5 - 2 = 3$, and $5 - 3 = 2$). We also played the 'Diffy' activity. (See page 59, Figure 9.)

But all the children except Jenny at Makewell had difficulty with written subtraction. To give them a new start I introduced 'shop-keeper's addition', using real money. From my work with the younger groups I realized that recording would be a stumbling block, and suggested that the first records should be only of the change. I extended the range of examples, and the children used a number line and ten-strip. However Ella and Margaret at Melia first gave the answer to $73 - 37$ as 44. They found the transition to harder examples too difficult; I needed more time, and more frequent sessions, to make the method permanent. But Steve, at Makewell, invented his own way of recording.

For 43 − 17 he wrote:
$\cancel{10}$ 3   My recording was: $17 + 3$
$\cancel{10}$ $20 + 10$
10                              $30 + 10$
10                              $40 + 3$
3   43
―――――   ―――――
26   26

Suddenly Steve saw how his method resembled mine. He was jubilant. Jenny at Makewell gave a clear explanation of her method (slaughtering figures).

$$^3\cancel{4}^{1}3$$
$$- 1|7$$
$$\overline{\quad 2|6}$$

She had recently been promoted to a higher set for mathematics and resented attending my sessions. She asked: 'Why do I have to come when there are several less brainy than I am?' Gladys, at Makewell, was also reluctant to attend my sessions after she was promoted.

I spent a considerable time helping the children to acquire the concepts of multiplication and division, to recognize the type of problems which required multiplication or division for their solution, and to understand why it was useful to memorize multiplication and division facts. Several of the children managed to multiply two-digit numbers by single digits, but multiplication by two-digit numbers was beyond all of them. I was unable to help them to overcome their difficulties in the time available.

Their first problem was with multiplication by ten. Until they could accept, for example, that 56 × 10 was 56 tens and that there were no units, they could not immediately record 56 × 10 = 560. The next problem was caused by the children's inability to recall the relationship between multiplication and addition. When I asked the children at Missingham to calculate 56 × 12 Allen said: '12 = 10 + 2. Let's find 56 × 10 and 56 × 2.' When this was done they all, without exception, tried to multiply the answers. When I reminded them that Allen had said: '12 = 10 + 2', so that to find the answer to 56 × 12, 56 × 10 and 56 × 2 had to be added, Allen himself asked, 'Why add when we are multiplying?' Arthur, at Meakins, also protested: 'But I thought we were multiplying.' This made me realize that these children needed far more experience of using ten-sticks and units for multiplication, and of making a written record of what they had done, before attempting two-digit multiplication.

Yet all the children accepted that one aspect of division was repeated subtraction. At Missingham, after they had solved the problem 'Have I enough shells in my bag for everyone in this group to have three each?' by taking three each, Allen said: 'So division really is subtraction.' At the next session I asked them to record (in symbols) what happened to my collection of 18 shells as each of the six children took three. They recorded:

$$18 - 3 - 3 - 3 - 3 - 3 - 3 = 0.$$

The next problem I gave the group at Missingham was: 'It is 40 days to Christmas; how many weeks and days is this?' Allen suggested: 'Subtract seven days at a time.' They did so, but they were not sure enough of the subtraction facts, so this took time. Tracy was first with the answer because she counted on her fingers. Before they had finished Allen said, 'I'm going to start again and subtract 14 days at a time – it's quicker'.

$$
\begin{array}{rl}
40 & \\
-7 & \quad \text{1 week} \\
\hline
33 & \\
-7 & \quad \text{1 week} \\
\hline
26 & \\
-7 & \quad \text{1 week} \\
\hline
19 & \\
-14 & \quad \text{2 weeks} \\
\hline
& \text{5 days, 5 weeks} \\
\hline
\end{array}
$$

Meanwhile Robert said: 'Why not take away 35 days? That's even quicker.' He recorded:

$$
\begin{array}{rl}
40 & \\
-35 & \quad \text{5 weeks} \\
\hline
& \text{5 days, 5 weeks} \\
\hline
\end{array}
$$

Tracy then suggested that we should find out how many weeks and days it would be if Christmas were 80 days from now. If I had anticipated this development I would have given the children practice in multiplying numbers by ten, in the hope that this might suggest subtracting 70 days (ten weeks) first. After wrestling with the subtraction of 14 days at a time, Robert said: 'It would be easier if we subtracted 70 days straight away.' But Tracy protested that this muddled her.

Robert recorded:

$$
\begin{array}{ll}
80 \text{ days} & \\
-70 \text{ days} & 10 \text{ weeks} \\
\hline
10 \text{ days} & \\
-7 \text{ days} & 1 \text{ week} \\
\hline
3 \text{ days} & 11 \text{ weeks} \\
\end{array}
$$

This happened at the final session. The children required far more practice for this method of long division to be retained over a period.

The four operations were applied to fractions also. At Missingham the children were having difficulty in halving odd multiples of ten. So I suggested that they should rewrite these multiples, for example: $70 = 60 + 10$, $90 = 80 + 10$. Suddenly Allen's face lit up as he exclaimed: 'I see now why you asked us to write numbers like this. It's to help us to find that half 70 is half 60 and half ten. That's 35.'

At the fourth session at Melia Ella asked if I would help them with fractions. She said, 'We've been doing fractions in class for three weeks but we still don't know what a fraction is'. I asked her to give me an example of what she was doing. She replied, '$1 - \frac{1}{4}$ and others like that'. The other children agreed that they did not understand what they were doing. I then asked how their teacher had begun fractions. 'She folded a circle of paper in four', Ella answered. Unfortunately, I also only had sheets of paper to hand, instead of the identical glasses of water I prefer to use. I cut some identical strips of paper and gave each of them two strips and two sheets of paper. I asked them to divide one strip of paper into four equal parts. 'How many parts are there in the paper strip?' I asked. I explained that each part was called one quarter of the whole strip, and that was written as $\frac{1}{4}$ (one part out of four). They labelled each part $\frac{1}{4}$, and labelled the unfolded strip 'one whole strip'. They then repeated the folding and labelling with a sheet of paper. This time the unfolded sheet was labelled 'one whole sheet'. I asked them to cut off one quarter from the strip. 'How much is left?' I asked. They all said 'Three quarters'. 'How do you think we write three quarters?' I continued. They all wrote $\frac{3}{4}$. I then asked them to record in symbols what they had done. They found this difficult until I asked them which operation cutting off a quarter was. We repeated this activity using the sheet of paper. Each time I asked them to put the remaining cut section on top of the whole strip or sheet so that they could check their answers. We also used the strips and the sheet to find fractions equivalent to $\frac{1}{2}$. We divided a third sheet of paper into eighths so that we could extend the range of equivalent fractions. They had no difficulty in stating the correct fractions when sections were removed, and they began to find recording easier. At the fifth session Mick, who had not seemed to be listening at the previous session, described how he would solve $\frac{1}{2} - \frac{1}{4}$, 'because $\frac{1}{2}$ is $\frac{2}{4}$ you see'. When I tried this work with the other groups I found that none of them had ever been given introductory practical activities with fractions. Yet all were able to halve and quarter a glass of water (other identical glasses were available) and a lump of clay (balance scales were provided). My work with these children caused me to provide the teachers with practical activities in fractions and to ask them to record each situation in symbols. The teachers, too, had some difficulties at the working sessions.

III. Findings from these sessions

1. The children at Melia achieved a standard higher than that of any other group, mainly because their attitude throughout the sessions was so positive.

2. Many children successfully systematized the number facts I helped them to learn during the two terms I was working with them.

3. Some of the children gained enough confidence to make more than one suggestion for solving the activity-based problems I set them.

4. Few of the children, even the oldest, were able, by the end of the two terms, to carry out written calculations without considerable help. The percentages of third and fourth-year children who were able to do written calculations with two-digit numbers were: addition, 70%; subtraction, 30%; multiplication, 15%; division, 0%. After four

and a half hours a week of learning mathematics, over a period of seven years, this achievement does not seem good enough. Most of the teachers of these children aimed only at making them efficient at written calculations in the four operations.

5. Some of the children, especially the fourth years, began to ask me to help them with specific topics with which they had difficulty during the week. Unlike the children at first schools they expected to understand what they were doing. Their increase in confidence became very noticeable and they were determined to do as well as they could. They began to adopt a mature attitude to their work.

IV. The fourth years – a special case

Background

I have already referred to the anxiety expressed by the fourth years at the middle schools when anticipating their transfer to a high school. The extent of the anxiety some of these children felt about the coming transfer is epitomized by the comment of one hard working slow-learning girl who talked to me about this: 'There will be no one to look after *us*. The teacher will write $x - 5$ on the board and there will be no one to tell us what x is!' Although I told her that I had worked with many of the children at the high school to which she was being trans-ferred, and knew most of the teachers, I could not allay her fears.

Until the fourth year the large majority of the slow-learning children showed no interest in mathematics, had a scant knowledge of any number facts and had little understanding of or skill in written calculations. But by the time they were twelve years old there had been a marked improvement in all these aspects and some increase in confidence, although many children continued to have difficulty with written calculations. What is the reason for this spurt? It does seem that we try to teach formal written calculations before these children understand them.

In the nine sessions I had with them, we could not make up all the ground these children had lost, particularly in written calculations, but it was encouraging to secure their goodwill (in contrast to some of the third years in the same group) and to capitalize the efforts they made.

CHAPTER FIVE

Conclusions from the project and some recommendations for work in mathematics with slow learners

I. The extent to which my aims were achieved

A. Enjoyment

The necessary change in the attitude of the children from dislike of mathematics to enjoyment was slow to materialize. First of all their prejudice against using materials for learning mathematics had to change. They did not at first regard activities and games as 'proper maths'. They knew that their more successful peers worked from books and did not use materials with their teachers. I had to assure them that I provided materials for *all* the children I taught – not just for them. I explained that learning mathematics by using materials took longer, but that they were more likely to remember what they had learned. They also had to accept that practising written calculations which they did not understand was a waste of time.

It took a long time for the younger children to enjoy the activities and games I gave them – and to say so. Many of them became apprehensive whenever I introduced a new activity. When I asked the middle groups (aged 8 to 10) what they meant by 'proper maths' they replied, 'Maths is sums'. It was hard to convince them of the progress they were making towards understanding what they were doing. They were sometimes unwilling to repeat an activity because they were afraid that they would not get it right a second time. In contrast, the oldest children often showed pleasure in what they were doing and in their achievements.

There were, of course, other factors which resulted in a more speedy change of attitude towards mathematics. The skill, personality and confidence of the teacher had a great influence on the amount of effort slow-learning children were willing to exert to learn it. A change of teacher sometimes worked wonders. Two ten-year-old girls at Movehall, who had not known the symbols for any of the mathematical operations, asked me one day 'to test our number facts'. A new teacher had motivated the children by taking them on a school journey during which they made maximum use of mathematics. This had made them aware of why they needed to learn mathematics and, at the same time, aware of their own deficiencies. They continued, 'We've learned a lot this term and we know why we have to learn so much'. In half a term they had memorized many essential addition and subtraction facts, had come to understand which of the four operations to use in a given situation, and could apply the appropriate language patterns. When I congratulated the two girls and their young teacher on this achievement the girls added, 'Our new teacher makes everything so interesting. The school journey made us see why we have to learn mathematics.' Perhaps motivating the children is the most important single factor in securing their cooperation.

B. Confidence

The majority of the slow-learning children gained in confidence as the sessions progressed, particularly the older ones. But if they measured success solely in terms of their ability to carry out written calculations successfully they were sometimes disappointed. It was difficult to persuade them that achievement could also be measured by the extent of their understanding of mathematical concepts. I also found it difficult on some occasions, despite my long experience, to ask the kind of question which would help the children to succeed (i.e. take the next step) without directly telling them the answer. I had to be particularly careful not to discourage them by asking a question which was too difficult for them at that stage. The question had to be one they could answer and which would make them feel that they themselves were taking a step forward.

C. Oral discussion

It took time to accustom the children to talking about what they were doing. They were afraid to commit themselves in case they revealed their lack of knowledge or of understanding. It was often difficult to teach them what the appropriate language patterns were and even more difficult to get them to apply the language patterns to what they were doing. I had to establish a routine in which the children worked in pairs, one telling the other exactly what to do. Even so, the younger children particularly needed more frequent practice than I could give them. I persuaded some teachers to undertake this work between my sessions but some of them became discouraged before the children had a firm grasp of the language patterns. These teachers could not believe that the activity/discussion stage could take so long.

D. Understanding the mathematical concepts

Nearly all the children appeared to acquire the concepts of place value (at least to two places), and of the four operations. Although the younger children became familiar with the problems which require one of the four operations for their solution (see M1, page 27), they were not ready for the transition to symbolic representation. Even the oldest children had difficulty in applying the two aspects of division (sharing and subtraction) to numerical situations.

For example: $20 \div 4$ as 20 divided into 4 equal sets (of 5) or
20 divided into sets of 4 (5 sets).

E. Seeing mathematics in action

All the children experienced mathematics in action and many realized the value of memorizing number facts. Some of the nine to 13-year-olds made a sustained effort to learn the number facts they used most often. They also tried hard to work out the facts they did not know from those they could recall easily. But I did not have time to help the older children to carry out written calculations in all the four operations successfully. They needed further help in the transition from using material and recording the calculation from the activity, to practice with abstract examples.

F. Appreciating that mathematics is concerned with patterns

Only those children who made sequences of enlarging squares, using unit squares, were able to discover number patterns for themselves. But all the children became familiar with the patterns of dots on dice and dominoes, and recognized sets of pebbles when they made 'scatter patterns'.

With the exception of the more severely disturbed children all showed some improvement during the two terms of the experiment. Above all their attitudes to work changed as they gained confidence in their ability to understand mathematics, to carry out activities and to record their results.

Not surprisingly, most progress was made by the older groups, especially those in the fourth year of the middle schools. They realized the importance of understanding what they were doing and made strenuous efforts to memorize number facts. Some of them gained sufficient confidence to make suggestions for solving problems and were able to appraise different methods. The response of the older groups was in marked contrast to that of many children in the first schools who lacked confidence and found it impossible to retain number facts between the sessions. It seems probable that a good deal of the number work the first school children are expected to do is beyond the capability of slow learners. They are therefore condemned to recurrent failure and to the low level of performance which so dismayed those heads who attended my sessions with the children. It became evident that in many instances the teachers were not providing enough activities to ensure that the children understood, and they became bored by written calculations which were quite beyond them. On the other hand these children could have enjoyed work with shapes and with some of the measures. Activities of this kind were seldom in evidence in the classrooms.

II. Were the needs of the slow learners being met when they transferred to high schools?

I had already arranged to interview the children from the project schools during the first term after their transfer. I had sent lists to the two project high schools of the children with whom I had worked, with a note of those children who were most apprehensive. I wanted to discover how well the children were settling, whether they still had anxieties and to what extent their needs in mathematics were being met. The heads at both high schools were most cooperative and encouraging. I had, of course, already worked with some of the mathematics teachers during the first input of the project.

The slow-learning pupils at the high schools had various anxieties. Two of them were worried because they were in the lowest 'band'. One of them said, 'I did not understand about the bands until I asked one of my friends. I would like to do things more quickly.' (This girl had been in a mixed-ability class at her middle school.) But the other pupil, though anxious about being in the lowest band, said, 'The teacher takes us very slowly and the pace is just right for me. If I make a mistake, the teacher is kind and not very strict.' Although the boys seemed less worried than the girls about being in the lowest band, one boy said, 'I like the work here. It's just right – but I don't want to drop to a lower maths group [remedial group].' The girl who had shown most anxiety about the approaching transfer had also gained confidence. She said, 'I'm happy here. I like the teachers. I can do all the sums I'm given. The teacher explains on the board then leaves us to work from books. There's never any talking in maths.' But in other respects this girl had not made progress. For instance, she could tell the time but she had no idea how to calculate duration of time. (This topic was not included in the teacher's scheme.) Were this girl's needs really being met?

A slow-learning boy at the other high school had said at his first interview: 'I'm not really settled. I'm sometimes in trouble. When a teacher shouts at me I won't do what he says ... I like maths with Mr. .... You choose your own section and carry on with a friend. This is a good way of working – I like to work with someone.' (He was an only child.)

The third time I saw him there had been a marked change. He said: 'I'm happy here now. I like the subjects and games. In maths I've learned a good deal. I like fractions. I understand them – they're exciting. I didn't know a thing about them before.' The boy explained that a man (the advisory teacher for mathematics) 'came in with some coloured bricks and this made me understand'. This interview underlined, once more, the importance of providing material when children are acquiring concepts. But there was another reason for this boy's change of attitude to school. His mathematics teacher (in his first post) explained, 'I expected trouble from this boy at first. Now I trust him.'

In some ways the needs of the slow-learning pupils were being met. All had settled well. Most of them were anxious to succeed in what they believed mathematics to be: written calculations. Most of them were achieving this at a simple level and showed that they understood what they were doing. A few were achieving more than this. But few, if any, were being given experiences which would help them to solve simple problems. There were situations they should be meeting and problems (like calculating journey times) they should be capable of solving. But there was no teacher of the lower bands in either school who had attended the first input of the project. There had been no change in the teaching of first-year slow-learning pupils in content or in style.

III. Some recommendations for teaching mathematics to slow learners

A. Organization

(1) The two-year age range within the groups of slow-learning children with whom I worked exacerbated the wide variation between the mathematical capabilities and knowledge of these children, particularly of the older ones. It would be inadvisable, therefore, to organize permanent groups of these children with such an age range.

(2) These children should not always be taken on their own for mathematics. The presence of one or more abler children often enlivens the responses and encourages slow learners to make suggestions themselves.

(3) The mathematics coordinator should take some responsibility for the work of the slow-learning children whenever this is practicable. If she is able to work with them once a week over a period, she will familiarize herself with their particular problems and be able to advise or actively help her colleagues.

B. The importance of changing children's attitude to mathematics

Effecting a change in the children's attitudes towards learning mathematics is the first pre-requisite for improvement in mathematics. The following points seem important in this respect:

(1) The children need to appreciate why they have to learn mathematics. For this reason, they should *use* mathematics, at however simple a level, rather than practise calculations before they understand what they are doing.

(2) They need to be given encouragement whenever possible. If we try to avoid saying, 'That's wrong', or even, 'No', and instead ask the children to talk about what they have done, they usually discover

for themselves where a calculation or the solution to a problem went astray.

(3) Attractive materials should be provided to help the children to learn mathematics. They should be reminded that all children learn more successfully and make more creative suggestions when they work with material. But they should be allowed to decide whether they work with materials or not and to choose the materials they require. They should also be encouraged to record their results in an attractive way.

(4) We should try to put less emphasis on written calculations and more on investigations and the solution of problems. Electronic calculating machines should be available and we should encourage the children to use them, letting them experiment for themselves and questioning them so that they do not become frustrated. But it is still important to help children with written calculations, making sure that they understand what they are doing. They will rarely need to work with more than two-digit numbers.

(5) It usually acts as an incentive for children to keep a record of their progress, both of the activities they have completed and of the number facts they have memorized.

C. Content

(1) Most emphasis needs to be given to the acquisition of concepts and to the solution of problems, but memorization of number facts should also receive attention.

(2) When the children are acquiring complex concepts such as the four operations and their language patterns, or place value, they require frequent short practice periods (10 to 15 minutes a day).

(3) The activities planned should give the children oppor-tunities to experience mathematics in action. The purpose of each activity should be made clear to the children. Subsequent questioning is essential to discover the extent of learning which has taken place.

(4) The programme should comprise:

(a) activities and games to help children to acquire concepts such as counting the number of objects in a set, place value, all the measures such as volume and capacity, mass and weight; and to recognize the problem situations which require the use of one or other of the four operations for their solution;

(b) games to assist in the memorization of number facts;

(c) written calculations (checked by using electronic calculators);

(d) activities involving three-dimensional and two-dimensional shapes, discovering how they are alike and how different; making patterns which repeat by reflection, by rotation or by both; recognizing properties of common shapes, and their nets; scale; relationships between perimeter and area, and between surface area and volume;

(e) probability games and activities; associating these activities with addition, difference and multiplication tables.

IV. A list of some mathematical activities used with slow learners aged 7 to 12 years

A. Number patterns

Materials: packs of ten cards, each with one number symbol from 0 to 9; a wide variety of objects for sorting and counting; dice.

(1) Match the correct number of objects to each symbol (in jumbled order).

(2) Arrange the jumbled number symbols in number order.

(3) Recognize the patterns of dots on a die as numbers.

Make and describe patterns, using a specific number of objects. The description should be a complete statement, e.g. three and four and three make ten. Sometimes make and describe 'scatter patterns'.

(4) Teachers introduce (a) the addition symbol, when children can describe the symbol as meaning 'Put together and say how many there are altogether'; (b) the 'equals' symbol, when children can describe this as 'has the same total as'. Later on, they will understand the symbol as 'is equivalent to'.

B. Dice games

Materials: dice, interlocking cubes, square centimetre paper.

(1) Play with a partner. Throw a die in turn. At each throw take as many cubes as your score on the die. After three throws, who has the higher total score? *(If the children do not think of 'comparing towers' use the following activity.)*

(2) For three children. Arrange yourselves in order of height. (*To help them to see the need for a base line.*) Now, the shortest child is to stand on a chair. Why is this not fair when we are comparing heights?

(3) Throw two dice and add the scores. Record the total. (*If the children count the number of dots on both dice, continue as follows.*) Put the die with the smaller score on top of the other. (*This helps the child to count on the smaller score. Teachers should gradually ask the children to memorize the number facts required when adding the scores on two dice: 36 facts in all. Give short written tests as well as oral tests. Group the facts: doubles of numbers 1 to 6; adding 1 (then 2, 3) to numbers 1 to 6; reversals of all these facts, e.g. 1 plus 6 and 6 plus 1.*)

(4) Record the totals for ten throws of a pair of dice. Which total did you record most often? Least often? What is the highest possible total? The lowest possible? Can you get all the scores in between these two? Show me this with dice. Now make a record sheet on squared paper for all the possible totals when throwing a pair of dice. Write the totals in order, one in each square. Throw the dice and record the totals until you have to stop. Which total 'won'?

(5) On squared paper make an addition square for the numbers 1 to 6. (Table 1, page 23). Which number occurs most often in the table? How many times does 7 occur? Record how many times each number occurs. What is the same about this table and your experiment when you were adding the scores on two dice?

(6) Throw two dice. Find and record the difference between the scores each time. (Find how many more one score is than the other.) Repeat the stages in activity (4), this time recording the differences: $6 - 4 = 2$. (Table 2, page 24).

(7) Take ten (interlocking) cubes. Make two equal towers with them. Then with your ten cubes make pairs of towers, one taller than the other. How many more cubes are there in the taller tower? Tell me what you have done. (*Teachers need to establish the language pattern: I have 6 red cubes, and 4 blue cubes. I have 2 more red than blue. If necessary, reinforce the need for a base line B(2).*) How many different pairs of towers can you make? Arrange all the pairs of towers in order, from the least difference to the greatest difference. Record the differences.

($5 - 5 = 0, 6 - 4 = 2, 7 - 3 = 4, 8 - 2 = 6, 9 - 1 = 8, 10 - 0 = 10$. *It is rare to get the final pair.*) What do you notice about the differences? (*If the children say, 'They are all even numbers', ask: 'What number would you start with to get odd differences?' If they do not know even and odd numbers, try activity C(1).*)

(8) Multiply the scores on two dice and record your answers. After ten throws, tell me which numbers you will not be able to get. Why?

(9) (a) Write down the three pairs of opposite numbers on a die. What can you find out about the total of each pair? (b) What are the numbers opposite each of these on a die?

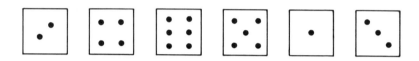

Figure 8

(c) Throw two dice. Record the numbers on the hidden faces and their total each time. Do this five times. What is your grand total?

C. Even and odd numbers; sampling

Materials: small pebbles, shells, etc.

(1) Is there an odd number of boys at school today? Of girls? Of children? How can we find out? (*Nearly all children suggest pairing and finding whether there is an odd man out. Vary the problems.*)

(2) Take a sample of pebbles. Without counting, find whether you have taken an odd or an even sample. Record odd or even. Put the sample back. Repeat, taking ten samples in all. How many samples were even? Odd? Did you have more evens than odds? Fewer evens than odds? The same number of odds and evens? Repeat this for another ten samples. Were your results the same? Find the totals for all 20 samples.

(3) Work in a group of four. Take ten samples each and record how many odds and evens you take. Find the totals for the group. If the number of odd and of even samples had been equal, how many would there have been of each? Which is nearer to this total, the

number of evens or of odds? Will the answer to this question always be the same?

(4) (*First teach the children the meaning of multiple.*) Take a sample of pebbles. Is your sample a multiple of three? How did you find out? Record whether the sample is a multiple of three or not. Put the sample back. Take ten samples in all, recording the result each time. Find the totals. Did you have more multiples of three or more non-multiples? Repeat this in a group of four, and find the totals. Why were there fewer multiples of three? What remainders did you get?

Repeat this experiment. This time record the remainders each time: 0, 1, 2. Find the totals for a group of four, each taking ten samples. What do you notice about the results for the whole class? Repeat, this time dividing each sample by four and recording the remainder.

D. Memorization of number facts

It is essential that the children should be able to memorize the addition and subtraction facts for the numbers 0 to 10 before proceeding to larger numbers. Activities and games should be attractive and varied (but can be a waste of time if not followed up). After any game, the teacher should give quick oral practice based on the number facts covered. This practice is partly to help the children to know which facts the game is designed to teach them, and partly to see how effective the game has been. Some children need to play a game many times before they can recall the number facts. Here are some examples of the games and activities I found successful.

(1) Material: Each child has a set of number cards 0 to 10.
(i) Put out pairs of cards with numbers whose sum is 10. Now reverse the numbers in each pair. Is the result the same? Repeat with other totals. (ii) Put out pairs of cards with a difference of 1 (2, 3, etc.). Record your results. (Make sure you record the numbers in the right order.)

(2) Use your set of cards for Snap. (*Two to four children.*) Share the cards and place these face down. The first to say Snap when a card is turned up which makes a total of 10 with a card already face up on the table takes all the cards on the table. (*Use a variety of totals and differences.*)

(3) A game for one or two children. Shuffle three or four sets of cards 0 to 10. Set out twelve cards face upwards. Cover any pair of

cards which add up to 10, using the next two cards from the pack. Continue until there are no cards left. Pair the top cards of each 'pack' which have a sum of 10. Make a written record of these pairs.

(4) Addition and subtraction trios. Take any two cards from the set, say 5 and 3. Find a card to complete:

(a) the addition trio (8, since $5 + 3 = 8$ and $3 + 5 = 8$);
(b) the subtraction trio (2, since $5 - 3 = 2$, and $5 - 2 = 3$).
   Record the trios. Return the cards to the pack, shuffle them and take two more cards. Complete the trios.

Play the trios game (*for two children*). Use two packs of cards, 1 to 10, well shuffled. One of you deals five cards each. Look at your cards. One of you puts down two cards. If your opponent can complete the trio he does so, announcing the trio and taking the 'trick'. If he cannot complete the trio, you may do so. Before the next turn, take cards from the pack so that you each have five cards once more. If neither of you can complete the trio, the two cards are placed underneath the pack. Your opponent then puts down two cards for you to complete. (Remember that you must always have five cards in your hand before you put any down.) At the end of the game whoever has more tricks is the winner. Choose one trick each and record four number statements from the trick. (*It is useful for teachers to play with a pair at some time to make sure that the children are making the most of their hands.*)

(5) Picture puzzles. (See page 15 and Figure 5.) Here are a few examples:

(a) On blue numbers put cards which are one more. On red numbers put cards which are one less (e.g. on 8 put 7).
(b) Dice addition, e.g. $6 + 6$, $1 + 3$, etc.
(c) Red numbers: How many more to make 5?
   Green numbers: How many more to make 10?
(d) Addition of 10.
(e) Subtraction of 10.
(f) Addition of 9.
   Subtraction of 9.
(g) Multiplication (and division) by 10.
(h) Squares of numbers.
(i) Odds and evens. Sort the even and the odd numbers. On each even number put the next greater even number (and work in the same way for odd numbers).

(j) Find the difference between ....

(k) How many more is 7 than 5? etc.

(l) Multiplication and division. (i) How many sets of 3 in 21? (ii) 6 sets of 3 .... How many?

Teachers will use many more examples. These puzzles test understanding of language and concepts as well as number knowledge.

(6) The Diffy game. Draw a large diamond shape on a sheet of paper. Mark in the middle points of each edge (Figure 9). Write any four numbers fewer than ten, one at each corner. At the middle points write the difference between the two numbers at the ends of each line. Join the middle points in a different colour. Mark the middle points of the edges of this new shape. At each middle point write the difference between the two numbers at the ends. Continue like this until you have to stop. Why did you have to stop? How many different shapes did you draw? Choose different numbers and start again. Can you get more than seven shapes?

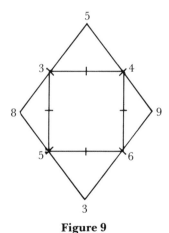

Figure 9

E. Place value

Materials: counting materials, including interlocking cubes; converted egg boxes; place value sheets.

(1) Take ten pebbles. Arrange them in sets of 2, 3, 4, 5.

What is your score? (I've five sets of 2 and zero ones, etc.) (*Change the initial number of pebbles.*)

(2) Use a converted egg box (see Figure 3, p.12) with two positions. Put your pebbles in the units compartment on the right. How many sets of 2 can you make? As you make each set, where will you put it? (Move it to an egg space to the left.) What is your score? Repeat, counting in threes, fours and fives.

(3) Today we are going to count in fours. But this is a secret so you must choose another name for four. You must not use that word. (Quad was chosen for four.) Start with your egg boxes empty. Each time I ring my bell I want you to put one pebble in the units compartment. (*Ring the bell three times, then ask for the score.*) What will you do when I next ring my bell? (We shall have quad units. We must move them to an egg space.) (*Ring the bell*). What is your score now? (One quad zero units.) (*Continue like this, asking for the score frequently, until it is 3 quads 3 units*). When shall we have to stop? (*If the children cannot tell you, repeat the activity, using interlocking cubes on a place value sheet. Each child makes his own place value sheet (Figure 4, page 12).*) This time call four 'pop'. When you have pop units, what will you do? (Pop them together and move the pop-stick to the left. My score is now one popstick zero units). (*Continue as before until the score is 3 popsticks 3 units*). What will happen when I ring the bell again? (*If the children do not answer, let them experiment to see what happens.*) (When you add one more unit you get quad units. So you move the quad to the left. Then you get quad quads, and you need another space to the left of the quads.) (*Repeat this activity daily, using different materials, and different counting numbers, fives and finally threes. Short practice sessions are important at this stage*). Do you understand why we use small counting numbers at this stage, and not ten?

(4) Use your egg boxes (or place value sheets). Start with a score of three sets of pent (5) and two units. How many units have you altogether? How did you find out? (I moved each set of pent in turn to the units section. I have 17 units.) (*Repeat this with other starting points and different counting numbers.*)

(5) Work in pops. On your place value sheets start with a score of three popsticks three units. At each sound from my triangle, remove one unit. (*Ask the score at frequent intervals, particularly when there are zero units.*) When the score is three popsticks zero units, what will you do at the next strike? (Move a popstick to the

units compartment. Break it into units; remove one unit.) (*Continue until the score is zero zero. Repeat this activity many times with different starting points and different counting numbers.*)

(6) Extension of place value. Material: multibase arithmetic blocks, dice. Play in pairs. Use base four material. Throw a die in turn.

(a) At each throw your opponent tells you what to do. At each throw, take as many unit cubes as the score on the die. When you have four unit cubes, what should your opponent tell you to do? (Change four units for one log.) If your opponent forgets to tell you to make a change, you can claim an extra turn. The first to complete a big cube is the winner. (*When a child says: 'Take one log one unit for a score of five', ask him to explain what he has said.*)

(b) Each of you starts with a big cube. This time you are going to subtract each die score. Remember to wait for your opponent to tell you what to do. Suppose you throw a score of four, what should your opponent tell you to do? (Change the big cube for four squares. Change one square for four logs. Remove one log which is four units.) The first to reach exactly zero is the winner.

(c) Take a pile of material. Can you make a big cube exactly?

(7) Material: interlocking cubes, dice, place value sheets. Play in pairs. This time you are going to count your score in tens.

(a) Throw the die in turn. At each throw take as many cubes as your score on the die. When you reach 10 (or more) move one set of 10 to the left. The first to score 30 or more is the winner. Record your total in two ways (e.g. 30 + 2 = 32).

(b) Start with a score of three tens. This time subtract your die score at each throw. Wait for your opponent to tell you what to do. (e.g. move one ten-stick to the right and break it into units. Remove – units.) The first to reach exactly zero is the winner.

(8) Material: small pebbles or other counting material.

(a) Take a collection of pebbles and estimate the number you have taken. Pattern your collection in tens and units so that I can see, at a glance, how many you have taken. How near was your estimate?

(b) Take a collection which you estimate to be 30 (40, 50, etc.).

Pattern your collection in tens and units. How near were you?

(9) Material: an abacus (two-spike) and beads of two colours to fit them, or interlocking cubes of two colours and a place value sheet. Dice.

(a) Play in pairs. Throw the die in turn. Your opponent will tell you what to do. This time you exchange ten unit beads for one bead of another colour (one ten-bead) before you put it on the next spike to the left. The first to get three ten-beads on the ten-spike is the winner.

(b) Start with three ten-beads. This time you are going to subtract your die score in units at each throw. Wait for your opponent to tell you what to do. The first to reach exactly zero is the winner. (*Later on, this game should be repeated, using beads of one colour.*) Record your final score.

(10) Material: three dice of different sizes.

(a) Use two dice of different sizes. When you throw both dice, the larger die gives you the score in tens, the smaller die the score in units. Throw the dice six times. Each time record your score in tens and units. Then arrange the scores in order from highest to lowest, in two columns. You score one point for each ten. What is your total? The highest possible total? The lowest possible total?

(b) *Extend to three dice of different sizes when the child is ready. Ask him to explain how he put the numbers in order. This time he will score one point for every hundred.*

(11) Material: strips of centimetre squared paper 100 centimetres long, two centimetres wide, coloured pens.
Work in pairs. Use your number lines to measure, and to record, the following body lengths (to the nearest centimetre): the perimeters of your head, face, foot, waist, neck, wrist and ankle. Arrange these lengths in order from longest to shortest. Work out the differences between each pair of these lengths. (This can be done by using the number lines.) Discuss your findings.

F. The four operations

(1) Discovery of number facts between 10 and 100. Material: ten-sticks and units, number lines, place value sheets.

(a) On your place value sheets put out a number of units fewer than 10. Record the number. Add 10 and record again. Continue to add 10, recording the new number each time until you reach the nineties. What do you notice? (The number of units remains the same. The number of tens increases by 1 each time.)

(b) Represent in ten-sticks and units a number in the nineties. Record this number. Subtract 10. Record the new number. Continue to subtract 10 until you have to stop, recording each time. Why do you have to stop? (The last number is fewer than 10.)

(c) Start with a number fewer than 9 on your place value sheet. Record this number. Add 9. Can you do this by first adding a ten-stick? What do you then have to do? (Take one unit away.) Continue to add 9, recording the new total each time, until you reach the nineties. What do you notice?

(d) Start with a number in the nineties. Arrange this number in ten-sticks and units on your place value sheet. Subtract 9. Can you do this by first subtracting a ten-stick? What do you then have to do? (Put one unit back.) Continue to subtract 9, each time recording the new number until you have to stop. Why do you have to stop? (*Other number facts, for example, doubles and near-doubles, can be discovered by the children themselves, using ten-sticks and units.*)

(2) Written recording of the four operations. Materials: ten-sticks and units.

(a) Addition of two-digit numbers, e.g. 47 + 35. Use ten-sticks and units to do this addition. Write down what you did.

$$47 \longrightarrow 40 + 7$$
$$\text{add } 35 \longrightarrow \underline{30 + 5}$$
$$70 + 12 \rightarrow 70 + 10 + 2 \rightarrow 80 + 2 \rightarrow 82$$

(b) Subtraction. Method (1): Shopkeeper's addition. Material: Coins up to £1.

(i) Find the change from £1 after spending 68p. The 'shop-keeper' counts out the change. The children record:

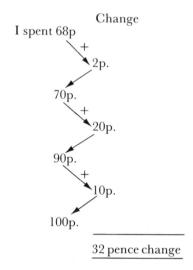

32 pence change

(ii) 'Abstract' examples. Material: a number line and ten-sticks to fit.

73 − 36

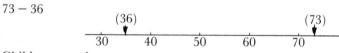

Children record:

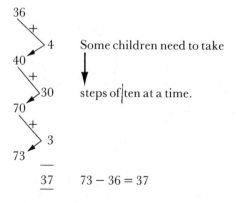

Method (2): Expanded notation. Material: ten-sticks and units. Use ten-sticks and units to calculate: 73 − 38.

$$73 \to 70 + 3 \to 60 + 13 \quad \text{(Change a ten-stick for}$$

Subtract $\quad 38 \to 30 + 8 \to 30 + 8 \quad$ ten units).

$$\overline{30 + 5 \to 35}$$

(c) Multiplication (by a unit number). Use ten-sticks and units and record what you did.

$$26 \times 3 \to 20 + 6$$
$$\underline{ \times 3}$$
$$60 + 18 \to 60 + 10 + 8 \to 70 + 8 \to 78$$

(d) Division. (*It would be preferable to begin by using ten-sticks and units.*)
Problem: It is 40 days to Christmas. How many weeks and days is this?
The children will make suggestions and try to carry these out. For example: subtract seven days (one week) at a time; subtract 14 days at a time; subtract 35 days at a time. When the number of days is to be increased to more than 70, give the children prior practice in multiplying numbers by 10, so that, when they are asked for an easy multiple of 7, they are likely to suggest multiplying by 10. For example, 'How many weeks and days is 83 days?' will be solved:

$$
\begin{array}{lll}
83 \text{ days} & & \\
-70 \text{ days} & 10 \text{ weeks} & \\
\hline
13 \text{ days} & & \\
-7 \text{ days} & 1 \text{ week} & \\
\hline
6 \text{ days} & 11 \text{ weeks} & 11 \text{ weeks } 6 \text{ days} \\
\hline
\end{array}
$$

G. Fractions

Materials: identical sheets and strips of paper (or lengths of ribbon or tape); identical plastic glasses; plasticene; balance scales. First find one half, then one quarter, of a strip of paper, a glass of water, a sheet of paper and a lump of plasticene. Label each part in two ways; for example, one half, ½. Label a second strip, a full glass, etc., as one whole strip, one whole glass. Use the materials to find fractions equivalent to half, one whole. (*Later on, extend the fractions to include eighths.*)

From a whole strip of paper divided into eighths, cut off three-eighths. What fraction is left? Record what you have done. Repeat this activity with a sheet of paper, a glass of water, etc.

CHAPTER SIX

Activities used with able children in first schools and some of their responses

I. Introduction

It was mainly in depth and in the range of problems which they were able to solve that the content of the sessions differed from that for slow learners of the same age. At first even the able children were apprehensive about what might be expected of them but, with the exception of the youngest girls (seven-years-old) at Frame, they soon came confidently to the sessions and grew accustomed to discussing and appraising the different methods they used to solve problems.

The younger children in the groups were sometimes at a considerable disadvantage because of their insecure knowledge. This was especially noticeable with the third year girls at Frame. After the third session, Sonia and Lucy, who had been so shy that they avoided answering questions whenever possible, remained after the session at their own request, to help me pack up. I asked them why they were too worried to answer any of the questions I posed. Sonia replied, 'We're waiting for you to put a cross on our work'. I asked, 'What makes you think I would do this? I never have done.' Sonia said, 'But our teacher always puts a cross on our work. It means, "You've got it wrong. Do it again". But when we ask her for help she tells us to go away and think. How can we ever get it right without help?' I assured the two girls that I would never mark their work with a cross and that I would not give them activities they could not do. (They went away singing, but this mood of reassurance did not last.) When I told their teacher about this conversation, she could not understand why her procedure should worry the children. The girls gradually became more forthcoming but they were never completely relaxed.

II. Content

A. General number activities

The first activity I gave to each group was estimating the number of pebbles in a collection, and checking their estimate by organizing a count in tens and units. I asked the children at Frame how they could make a good estimate rather than a wild guess. Christine suggested, 'Halve the collection and count one half, then double it'. David said, 'Quarter it, count a quarter and times that by four'. They did this, and counted each quarter, 'just to check'. The total was 113, but the third years did not know how to write numbers greater than 100 and recorded 10013.

The children at Fleet did not know how to find the difference between their written estimate and the actual (patterned) total, until one of them decided to use pebbles to make a patterned collection of pebbles to represent their estimate. They then found the difference by matching.

B. Odds and evens

Most of the children were already familiar with even and odd numbers. (However, Kathryn at Flanders suggested that when they were throwing a pair of dice and adding the scores, seven occurred most often 'because it's even'.) The children at Foster were so quick at recording the number of evens and odds from ten samples of pebbles that I suggested they should take another ten samples and find how many were multiples of three. As soon as they started, Charles said, 'I've got remainders of one and two this time'. 'Then could you record your results in a different way?', I asked. Charles suggested that we could record the remainders in columns: 0, 1, 2. Meanwhile, Joan had found the totals for the evens and odds activity. She said, 'I've got 46 evens and 44 odds. Shouldn't these both be 45? I think evens and odds should be equal. Have I made a mistake?' Joan's question led to a discussion about the difference between our limited experiment and Joan's theory that odds and evens ought to occur the same number of times. Some of the children compared their own results for 20 samples with the totals for the group.

C. Dice games

(1) Once more, none of the children knew that the sum of the numbers on opposite faces of a die was always the same: seven. I asked the children at Fleet what operation they could use on the pairs of numbers on opposite faces of a die to get the same result for each pair. Peter said, 'Add them and you get seven each time'. He was also the first to suggest multiplying seven by three to obtain the sum of the numbers one to six. But Jill, in the same group, did not know three sevens. She described the method she used, 'I know that 6 and 6 are 12. So I added 2 more to get 7 and 7, 14. I added 6 to get 20, and 1 to make up the third 7.'

(2) I asked the children to throw two dice 20 times, and to record the difference between the scores each time. At Foster we returned to this activity after a gap of three weeks. The children could not remember which operation they had used on the two scores. Charles volunteered, 'I remember that we used two dice to get zero from two sixes'. Ian then said, 'So we must have been taking away'. There was general agreement. I therefore asked the children to make a 'difference' table (Table 2, page 24) for the numbers one to six. (We found differences instead of subtracting, to avoid the use of negative numbers.) I asked them to describe the numbers in the bottom row. 'We're adding one each time', Ivor said. 'What is happening in the top row?', I asked. 'We're taking away one each time', Joan answered. I then asked them to describe the numbers in the fourth row. Richard replied, 'We started by taking one away each time. Then we added one. 3, 2, 1, 0, are in order, so are 0, 1, 2.' 'Now tell me about the columns', I said. Jean answered, 'Column six starts at 5 and goes down 1 each time to 0. The first column starts at 0 and goes up 1 each time to 5.' 'What about the diagonals?', I asked. Charles said, 'One diagonal is all zeros. The other one starts at 5 and goes down in 2s to 1, then up in 2s. The numbers are all odd.' 'There's patterns everywhere', the children concluded.

On another occasion, I asked these children to throw two dice and to record the product of the scores each time. 'What are the highest and the lowest possible scores?', I enquired. These were soon identified as 36 and 1. 'Can you get all the numbers in between by

M2

From the table of differences (Table 2, page 24) we can find how many times each difference (range 0 to 5) occurs. (Table 4).

Table 4

Difference	0	1	2	3	4	5
Frequency in Table 2, page 24	6	10	8	6	4	2

If we had made a subtraction table instead of a difference table the results would, of course, be different. This time some of the subtractions are negative. For example, in row one, we have subtracted each number (1 to 6) in turn from 1. The results are entered in the first row. $(1 - 1 = 0, 1 - 2 = -1, 1 - 3 = -2, ...)$ (You may like to make a subtraction table for yourself, see Table 5.)

Table 5: Subtraction of pairs of numbers 1 to 6

6	5	4	3	2	1	0
5	4	3	2	1	0	−1
4	3	2	1	0	−1	−2
3	2	1	0	−1	−2	−3
2	1	0	−1	−2	−3	−4
1	0	−1	−2	−3	−4	−5
−	1	2	3	4	5	6

The frequency of occurrence of each subtraction possibility in Table 5 is shown in Table 6.

Table 6

Subtraction result	0	±1	±2	±3	±4	±5
Frequency in Table 5	6	5	4	3	2	1

There is an obvious pattern in the frequencies of subtraction Table 6. Can you find an axis of symmetry in Table 5? (It is one of the diagonals.)

multiplying dice scores?', I asked. 'No', Charles said, 'You couldn't get 17, nor any multiple of 7 because dice do not have 7 on them'. They continued to work at this until they were satisfied that they had finished. I then asked them to make a multiplication square for the numbers one to six, but the younger children did not know the table of threes (and one of them did not know that $6 \times 3 = 3 \times 6$), so this took longer than I had anticipated.

Table 7: Table of products of the set 1 to 6

6	6	12	18	24	30	36
5	5	10	15	20	25	30
4	4	8	12	16	20	24
3	3	6	9	12	15	18
2	2	4	6	8	10	12
1	1	2	3	4	5	6
×	1	2	3	4	5	6

When they had finished, we compared the frequency with which the products occurred in the multiplication square (Table 7) with the frequency in the experimental results. I asked them, 'What has the multiplication square to do with multiplying the scores on two dice?'. After some thought, Charles said, 'The numbers on the dice are the same as the numbers we multiplied to make the table'. 'Does the table contain all the products of pairs of numbers from the set 1 to 6?', I asked. 'Yes', Ian replied, 'because the numbers 1 to 6 are in order in the table'. This was the first occasion in the course of the project on which I received a complete answer to this question.

D. Place-value activities

(1) I had already found that some of the third years could not write three-digit numbers correctly. To help me to discover the extent of each child's understanding of place value, I taught them two place-value games. The children played in pairs with a well-shuffled pack of cards, comprising two of each of the numbers 1 to 9, placed face down. Each child in turn took one card and placed it in one of the columns on a place-value sheet (Figure 2, page 12). I had explained that the

higher two-digit number would win. When each took a second card, this had to be placed in the empty column. Each child then said his score aloud. If the child with the higher number could say by how many he had won, he scored two points. (Number lines were available to help children with this subtraction.) After five games the winning score was reversed: the child with the lower number was the winner.

In the second game, called 'Racing to 100', the number of cards taken (one at a time) was extended to three. The cards could be placed either in the same column or in different columns. The winning score was the score nearest to 100, above or below. This time both children scored a point if they could say how far their score was from 100. There was a bonus point for 'hitting the jackpot'!

These games helped me to assess not only each child's understanding of two- and three-digit numbers but also his facility with the subtraction of such numbers.

(2) It was during the course of the place-value games that each child made a 100-unit number line (a metre long, so that it could also be used as a tape measure). Again, the youngest children sometimes made unexpected mistakes. For example, Elsie at Fowler labelled the 40 mark as 14. I suggested that the children should check their labelling by finding the halfway mark and also one quarter and three quarters of the number line. They all did this, without hesitation, by folding. There were many slips; at Finlay, only Joseph had labelled the line correctly. (They marked the tens in one colour, the fives in another, and left the units unmarked.) Each then measured, and recorded, various body lengths such as the height and reach, and the perimeters of the head, neck and waist. After the children had arranged these measurements in order of length, I asked them to record which of these was nearest to one metre, half a metre and a quarter metre; and also which two measurements were nearest to each other. Despite the slips all the children enjoyed this activity. Moreover, I could assess the facility they showed in manipulating numbers as they worked the necessary subtractions and divisions. For example, they doubled their neck measurement and found how close this was to their waist measurement, and halved their waist measurement to compare this with their neck perimeter.

E. Extension of place-value to 3 and 4 positions

Since some of the children were unsure about writing three-digit numbers, particularly between 100 and 110, I decided to use multibase arithmetic blocks to extend their knowledge of place-value. Using base four and a die, pairs of children first played 'Build a cube', then 'Break a cube'. Very few had seen the material before, so after persuading them to build first the tallest tower and then the factory which occupied the greatest floor space, I asked them to name the four pieces. The names most children suggested are shown in Figure 10.

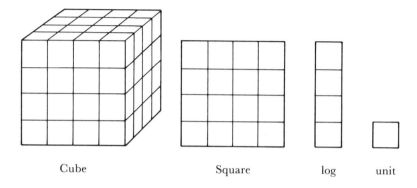

Cube   Square   log   unit

Figure 10

Many of the children immediately compared the material with our own place-value system. For example, Sonia at Frame exclaimed, 'It's like hundreds, tens and units'. Christine immediately pointed out, 'No, it's thousands, hundreds, tens and units'. The children soon noticed that four units made a log, four logs made a square and four squares made a cube.

I gave the children practice in using the language of exchange. At each throw of a die, the opponent had to tell the thrower exactly what to do. For example, if **⦂** was the score on the die the opponent said, 'Take 5 units. Change 4 units for a log. Your score is 1 log, 1 unit.' Of course these children soon took short cuts; for this score they usually said, 'Take one log, one unit'. When I questioned this instruction, Peter at Finlay explained, 'One log is 4 units; 1 more unit makes 5'. (If an opponent failed to notice a necessary exchange, the thrower could claim an extra turn. But these children rarely missed an exchange.) The winning goal for 'Build a cube' was, of course, exactly one cube. Later on, the children decided on their own goals. Then we reversed the game. Each child started with a cube and subtracted the score on the die in units. Some of the children repeated the games using base three, base five, and finally, base six, using two dice. When these children needed one unit only to complete a cube, they decided to build more than a cube and to subtract subsequent scores in the hope of finally getting one. Another group suggested that, when they were throwing two dice, they might use any operation at each throw, since 'this would be more fun'. I asked them in how many different ways they could get a score of 1 from two dice. They made several suggestions: $1 \times 1, 1 \div 1, 6 - 5, 5 - 4$, etc.

I next asked them how they could adapt the game in order to use base ten. They decided that their goal should be a square (100 units) and that they would use two or three dice and add the scores. Later on, they reversed the game; each child started with a square and subtracted successive scores until they reached zero (or fewer).

F. The four operations

While the children were playing games I had been able to introduce appropriate language patterns as well to assess their oral facility with addition and subtraction facts. Most of them became efficient at adding two 2-digit numbers mentally, but they continued to find the subtraction facts more difficult. I therefore introduced them to addition and subtraction trios, not only to help them to memorize the subtraction facts by associating these with trios of numbers, but also to emphasize the relationship between addition and subtraction.

At Finlay we began with trios whose sum was 10, because some of the able group were unsure about the bonds of 10. Neither Peter nor his younger sister Iris could tell me how far short of 100 their score of 98 was. They guessed 4?, 3?, 1? But once I had suggested that they should use a number line to help them, Peter said, 'My new score is 68. I need 32 to make 100. I said to myself, "68, two to make 70, 30 to make 100"'. These children were able to record four statements for each trio they made. For example, for 2, 8, 6, they wrote: $2 + 6 = 8$, $6 + 2 = 8, 8 - 2 = 6, 8 - 6 = 2$. Terry, at Flanders, suggested 5, 5, 10 as a trio. This time the children could find only two statements, 'because two of the numbers are the same'. 'Will you get only two statements for all trios with two numbers the same?', I asked. They tried 2, 2, 4; 3, 3, 6; and others. I asked them to find another trio for 5, 5. They suggested 5, 5, 0; it was some time before they were able to give all four statements. The children in all the groups enjoyed playing the trios game, which gave them further practice in completing number trios. The 'Diffy' activity focused attention on subtraction trios (see D(6), page 59).

At Fleet a different situation arose. When the children were working with the trio 3, 3, 6, Victor wrote: 3 − 6 = 9, and then corrected himself saying, 'No, I can't do it'. 'Yes, you can', Julia said. 'It's minus 3.' 'How do you know?', I asked. 'My Mum told me', Julia replied. (Her mother was not a teacher!) The boys were curious to know how Julia got her answer and what it meant, so we extended the number line backwards (Figure 11).

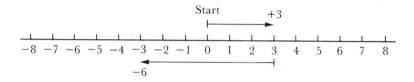

Figure 11

Julia explained, 'You walk three paces forwards and six paces backwards. So you arrive at minus three'. The children set examples for each other, walking up and down the number line, delighted with their discovery. Peter said, 'I'm going to try this on my teacher'.

To extend the concept of place-value and to help the children at Fleet to record addition and subtraction, I provided them with multi-base arithmetic blocks (base 4). Each child took some of each shape, remembering to take fewer than 4 of any shape. In pairs they found, and recorded, how much they had altogether, and the difference between the two amounts, exchanging the pieces as necessary. (At this stage they rarely forgot to convert from one piece to another.) I was interested to hear Richard, at Foster, who was using base 6, say to his partner, 'I've got 6 cubes. Let's call this new unit a big log.'

When we studied multiplication and division as abstract operations (instead of using them to solve problems), I tried to help the children to see the relationships between all four operations. For example, when each child at Flanders had arranged 12 pebbles in sets of 2, I asked them first to give me statements in words, then to write corresponding statements in symbols. Terry said, 'We've got six sets of 2'. All the children recorded this as: 2 + 2 + 2 + 2 + 2 + 2 = 12. Pressed by me, Terry remembered the symbol for 'times' and recorded $6 \times 2 = 12$. (The more correct recording would have been $2 \times 6 = 12$.)

When I asked the children to divide a set of 14 pebbles by 2, all except Peter, at Finlay, arranged the pebbles in sets of 2. Peter divided his collection into 2 sets and said, 'I'm sharing'. He recorded $14 \div 2 = 7$ (in each set). To help them to see that the other aspect of division is subtraction, I asked the other children at Finlay how they could find out how many sets of 2 pebbles I had in my hand. They said, 'Let's each take two pebbles and see how many are left'. 'So if I start with 14 in my hand, how could you record what you have done?', I asked. Peter wrote: $14 - 2 - 2 - 2 - 2 - 2 - 2 - 2 = 0$. I then asked them if they could use the division sign for this. After some thought John wrote: $14 \div 2 = 7$ (sets of 2).

To emphasize the two aspects of division we used multibase arithmetic blocks (base 4) again. Each child took a collection. I asked them to divide their collections by 2. They all did this by sharing. Some started with the cubes, and others with the units, the logs or the squares. When I asked them why they started as they did, John said he had looked to see where he had an even number of pieces, to avoid exchanging. 'Will you get the same answer wherever you start?', I asked. They tried starting with different pieces and decided that it was easier to begin with the largest pieces, the cubes, and continue systematically. They each wrote a record of their calculation.

When I suggested that they should try the subtraction aspect of division, they said that this would mean dividing into sets of 2. For this purpose they changed all the pieces into units. I was glad that the bell went before they had finished!

In the next session I gave them a different problem, 'How many models, each made from a square, a log and a unit, could you make from your own collection?'. At Frame they began, as before, to convert all the pieces to units until I asked them to make a model four times as large as the original. Lucy was the first to see that the large model must be one cube, one square and one log, 'Because 4 units make a log, 4 logs make a square and 4 squares make a cube'. After this discovery, they first made larger models, exchanging as necessary, until the amount left was less than would make another model of one cube, one square, one log. They then made the smaller models: one square, one log and one unit. Each large model scored four points; each small model scored one point.

G. Scale: squares

During the final two sessions, I was able to provide the children with a variety of investigations based on unit squares.

(1) At Flanders one class had set out a display of squares made with alternate unit squares in two colours. I asked the able group whether the same number of squares of each colour had been used for each of the larger squares. At first the children said, 'Yes'. Then they themselves began to make squares in alternate colours. They began with a 2 by 2 square. 'There's the same number of each colour in this square', they said. I suggested that they should make a record of the number of units of each colour used as they made larger squares. After a while Terry said, 'Odd squares have a different number of the two colours. Even squares have the same number of each colour.' I asked Terry what he meant by odd squares. 'Squares with an odd number of units on the edges', he answered. I continued, 'In your "odd" squares how are the numbers of the two colours different?'. 'There's one more of one of the colours', Terry said. 'What is the smallest square of all?', I asked. Terry looked at the sequence and then said, excitedly, 'It is just one square, and one's an odd number, so I've used one more of that colour'.

(2) The children at Frame had difficulty in calculating the number of unit squares they had used to make larger squares. Sohrab, who was convinced that 1×1 was 2, discovered while making a sequence of squares that 1×1 was just one square, the first in the sequence. As the children made bigger squares, I encouraged them to calculate the number of unit squares they had used, rather than to count the units one by one. When they built the 6 by 6 square none of them knew how many units they had used. Sohrab said, 'Three twelves must be the same as six sixes; so 6×6 must be 36'.

While Christine was trying to calculate the number of unit squares from the sequence the children had built, she made an interesting discovery. Instead of making a square she had made a rectangle 5 by 7. I asked her to change this into a square. As she did so, she said, 'I need one more unit to make the big square'. She continued to work at this problem. She made a 4 by 6 rectangle and again found that she needed one more unit to make the 5 by 5 square. Without making other squares she found that the rectangle 3 by 5 needed one more unit to make it into the 4 by 4 square, and the 2 by 4 rectangle needed one more unit to make it into the 3 by 3 square. She was excited by her discovery. I asked her how she knew which rectangles to start with, and how she knew the size of the square. Christine answered, 'The edges of the square are always in between the edges of the rectangle'. 'What rectangle would you make a 6 by 6 square from?' I asked. 'I'd start with a 5 by 7 rectangle and one more unit to make that square', Christine answered.

(3)   When I asked each child to take two handfuls of unit squares and to build the largest square they could, they all made square frames. When I asked them how many unit squares they had used, they looked at the edge of the square and multiplied this by four to obtain the answer. Oswald, at Flanders, was a very able boy but it was hard to convince him that his count of 28 units for his square frame with edge 7 was incorrect. All the members of this group found that they had used four fewer units than they had calculated from the number of units in the edge of the square. It was Kathryn who first said, 'I see. We've counted the corners twice.' The others agreed and began to work out the number of units they would need to make square frames of various edges. When I asked them to tell me how they were doing this they said, 'You multiply the number of units in the edge by 4, then take 4 away'. But Oswald said, 'I take away 1 first from the number of units in the edge, then I multiply by 4'. He drew a diagram to show us why he did this. Kate said, 'I've got another way. I say, "2 tens and 2 eights and add them, when the edge is ten".' She, too, drew a diagram. Thomas said, 'I take 2 units from the number of units in the edge, multiply by 4, then add 4'.

I hoped to help the children to suggest another method by focusing attention on 'the hole in the middle'. I asked the groups to describe the hole. Terry said, 'It's square. Its edge has two fewer units than the outside frame.' 'Does this give you another method for finding how many units you used for various frames?', I asked. There was no response, so I asked the children to tell me the size of the smallest frame. 'The smallest must be a frame of 3 by 3 with one unit square in the middle. The next one, 2 by 2, has no hole in the middle so it doesn't count', said Kathryn. However, the children at Foster included the 2 by 2 frame in their set of frames since it had a zero hole in the middle.

Excitement ran high during the final sessions. All the children had enjoyed the work with unit squares, although the majority of them did

M3

Christine found that: $\quad 7 \times 5 + 1 = 36\ (6^2)$
$6 \times 4 + 1 = 25\ (5^2)$
$5 \times 3 + 1 = 16\ (4^2)$
continuing the pattern, $\ 4 \times 2 + 1 = \ 9\ (3^2)$
$3 \times 1 + 1 = \ 4\ (2^2)$
$2 \times 0 + 1 = \ 1\ (1^2)$

Throughout the investigation Christine made a series of rectangles, each with one edge two units longer than the other. Each time she found that she needed one more unit to complete the square of the number between the two she had started with (the average of the two numbers). This is the general result Christine had discovered.

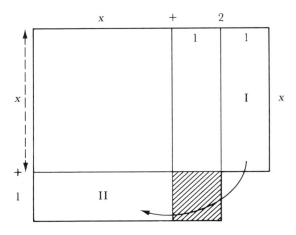

Figure 12

When the rectangle I (x by 1) is rotated in to its new position II one more unit is needed to complete the square on $x + 1$.

Take the original rectangle to have edges x and $x + 2$ units long.
The area of the rectangle is $x \times (x + 2)$ or $x^2 + 2x$
Christine added one unit, which gives $x^2 + 2x + 1$.
This is $(x + 1)\ (x + 1)$, or the square of $x + 1$.
Test for $x = 10$.
Area of rectangle $10 \times 12 = 120$ square units.
Add 1; 121 is the square of 11 (the average of 10 and 12).

not suggest as many methods of finding the number of unit squares in successive frames as had the children at Flanders. When I asked the children in each group how they felt about the sessions, they said they had enjoyed everything we did, but especially the games. (There was one exception. Kathryn at Flanders said that she liked doing sums best of all.) They had all come willingly and cheerfully to all the sessions despite the fact that they usually missed a recreational lesson in order to do so.

M4

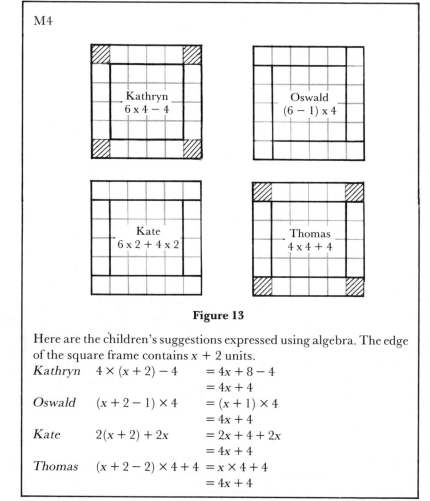

Kathryn
6 x 4 − 4

Oswald
(6 − 1) x 4

Kate
6 x 2 + 4 x 2

Thomas
4 x 4 + 4

Figure 13

Here are the children's suggestions expressed using algebra. The edge of the square frame contains $x + 2$ units.

Kathryn $4 \times (x + 2) - 4$ $= 4x + 8 - 4$
$= 4x + 4$

Oswald $(x + 2 - 1) \times 4$ $= (x + 1) \times 4$
$= 4x + 4$

Kate $2(x + 2) + 2x$ $= 2x + 4 + 2x$
$= 4x + 4$

Thomas $(x + 2 - 2) \times 4 + 4$ $= x \times 4 + 4$
$= 4x + 4$

III. Findings from the sessions

1. All the children had a good attitude both to mathematics itself, and to the activities we covered. Although a few of them were unaccustomed to working in a group (and some of them to working with materials), they adapted quickly to the new routine. They all became particularly interested in finding patterns in number.

2. The children made a variety of numerical mistakes which betrayed the fact that they were unable to recall essential number facts easily, although their teachers had given them considerable practice with written calculations based on such knowledge. However, the children were usually adept at working out the facts they did not know and in consequence most of the teachers were unaware of their ignorance. The children with the most extensive knowledge of number facts were at Flanders, one of the more traditional schools. Here the teacher gave them regular oral number practice and the children were quick and confident. It was possible to develop problems further with them because of their facility with numbers. However, the children who were least knowledgeable (even about addition facts) came from Fowler, another traditional first school. Not surprisingly, most of the able children performed better in short written tests than in oral tests (to which they were not accustomed).

3. The children often revealed individual weaknesses in number knowledge when they were working on activities such as making a number line, measuring various body lengths and comparing these. When they recorded the necessary calculations they also showed the extent of their understanding of the methods they used, as well as their facility with numbers.

4. In every able group there were one or two children, usually Asians, who were quicker than the rest. 'Because Dad gives me sums at home. My Dad gives me seven-figure sums, and I always get them right', Sohrab at Frame protested when I asked the children to find their total dice scores. I asked him to tell me the largest number he knew. 'A million', he said, without hesitation. 'How do you write a million?', I asked. 'One and five zeros', he said. At this stage I did not continue my questioning, as he had had no experience of large numbers in real situations.

5. Few of the children had been encouraged to find quick mental methods: for example, in the addition and subtraction of two-digit numbers. I realized that it was unlikely that the teachers would have

provided material to help the children to discover their own quick methods, but I was surprised to find how many children were handicapped in this way. I was also surprised to find that the first reaction of the able children when given a column of figures to add (for the score during a game) was to count on their fingers! However, they showed their potential by rapidly making suggestions for the quick addition and subtraction of 9, as soon as I provided them with ten-sticks and units. 'Take away ten and put one back', was the suggestion for quick subtraction of nine before anyone had done more than look at the material. Subsequently, in the repeated subtraction of 9 from 100, this suggestion was applied accurately.

It had been a pleasure to work with these children. Although, in the unaccustomed group situation, they were sometimes noisy, their interest never seemed to flag.

Activities used with children of ages 7 and 8

Slow learners	*Able children*
1. Number patterns pp. 7–8	1. Estimating, organizing and checking number of objects in a collection p. 68
2. Dice games: addition, difference pp. 8–10	2. Dice games: addition and difference p. 69
3. Sampling: odds and evens p. 11	3. Sampling, p. 68
4. Place value, pp. 11–15 using multibase arithmetic blocks p. 14	4. Place value, pp. 71–74
	5. Four operations: situations and language patterns; addition and subtraction trios, pp. 74–75 multiplication and division, pp. 75–76
	6. Number patterns: of squares, growth (multiplication) patterns, pp. 77–80

CHAPTER SEVEN

Activities used with able children aged 8 to 10 at middle schools, and some of their responses

I. Introduction

The achievement of these groups differed to a greater extent than that of the younger groups. Furthermore, the groups differed considerably in their attitudes towards mathematics. Some of them said how much they enjoyed the subject, others said how boring it was. Most of the children looked forward to the sessions, even when some of these had to be held at the end of the day. No one in these groups complained about missing recreational lessons. However, the children at Meakins were using a new workcard system with their teacher. Unfortunately, although the cards contained a wide variety of activities (in addition to a considerable amount of computational practice), they gave precise instructions about carrying out each activity. The children were rarely encouraged to take the next step for themselves. In consequence, some of these children were reluctant to tackle the problems I gave them, because they realized that I expected them to think out a solution for themselves. (Furthermore, this group contained an older disturbed boy whose behaviour was always conditioned by what had happened earlier in the day. He was often in trouble, and although he was very good at mathematics, he found it hard to concentrate on such occasions.)

From the outset I provided material which would help the children to solve the problems I set them. I explained that they could use the material whenever they thought it would help them – there was no compulsion. They were unaccustomed to using material but only one child remarked, 'Using dice is babyish'.

I encouraged the children in every group to make as many different suggestions as they could for solving the problems I provided. The suggestions were always made orally, and discussed; consequently, as the children became less inhibited, some of the sessions were noisy. One child would make a suggestion, another would react to the idea, which would often be discussed and developed by the whole group. Frequently, I tried to help the children to generalize the suggestions they made but they found this difficult.

In some of the groups there were more boys than girls. (In one group there were seven boys and only one girl.) Since, with one exception, the girls were quieter than the boys, I usually had to intervene from time to time to make sure that the girls had opportunities to contribute their solutions. They were always ready with one.

II. Content

I rarely needed to give these children either oral or written tests covering number knowledge. Individual weaknesses, usually among the first years, were revealed by the child's performance in the activities and games.

None of the children was familiar with all of the problem situations which require the use of one of the four operations for their solution. In consequence, they did not know the appropriate language patterns. But once we had studied the different situations, and I had established the language patterns, the children were quick to recognize similar situations and to use the appropriate phraseology for themselves.

I was able to introduce topics which I had not tried with children of the eight to ten-year-old age group before. From the outset I emphasized the importance of looking for number patterns and describing these in simple mathematical language. The topics included:

1.   (a) Addition and subtraction trios, (b) multiplication and division trios (leading to games).
2.   Probability: games with dice.
3.   Sampling: odds and evens; multiples of three, four, etc., recorded according to remainders after dividing by three, four, etc. Introduction of the concept of an average.
4.   The four operations: various situations which require the use of these operations. Fractions and decimals.

5. The properties of multiples of 2, 3, 4, 5, 8, 9, 10 and 11. (This led to a study of prime numbers.)
6. Scale. The properties of enlarging squares and cubes; number patterns associated with sequences of squares and cubes. Enlarging other three-dimensional shapes.
7. Properties of the shapes of containers. The concepts of area and volume and how these are measured.
8. Investigating the area of the cross-sections of plastic containers of different shapes with the same perimeter. (a) Finding what would be the largest possible area with a given perimeter. (b) Fixing the area of rectangles and investigating possible variations in the perimeter. Relating the patterns discovered to addition and multiplication tables.

A. Introductory number activities

By means of the addition and subtraction trios I was able to focus attention on the situations and the language patterns of the two different aspects of subtraction. The preparations for the game and the game itself helped the children to memorize addition and subtraction facts as trios; e.g. 3,5,8; 3,5,2.

The children at Melia were discussing alternatives to the statement: $3 + 4 = 7$. Ivor suggested $7 - 3 = 4$. 'What situation does this represent?', I asked. 'Seven take away three', was the reply. Charles said, 'Seven take away four; that's $7 - 4 = 3$'. 'These are both examples of one aspect of subtraction', I said. 'Can you think of a different subtraction situation?' Helena said, 'If I add four to three I get seven'. I persevered: 'Subtraction also comes from an entirely different situation. Use the word "more".' Stephen suggested: 'Three more than four is seven.' 'Begin with seven', I urged. Charles said, 'Seven less three is four'. Peter said, 'Seven is four more than three'. I said, 'There is another language pattern for the comparison of two sets. The word used begins with "d".' Finally, Peter suggested, 'Find the difference between seven and four'.

The children persisted in offering me subtraction 'sums' instead of subtraction problems because their initial experience had been based entirely on 'sums'. We therefore reviewed the different everyday problem situations which require the use of subtraction for their solution. This took time and I returned to everyday subtraction problems at frequent intervals.

I next explained that 3, 4, 7, was an addition trio and asked the children to write down the four addition and subtraction facts associated with this trio. They wrote: $3 + 4 = 7, 4 + 3 = 7, 7 - 3 = 4$ and $7 - 4 = 3$. The next trio they suggested was 4, 4, 8. They discovered that there were two statements only for this trio: $4 + 4 = 8$, $8 - 4 = 4$. Florence, at Missingham, first described such trios as 'double numbers which make a third'. She amended this to: 'two numbers which are the same and a third which is the sum of the two'. I then focused attention on the two addition and subtraction trios which could be made from any number pair e.g. 4, 6, 10 and 4, 6, 2. The children were surprised to find four statements for 3, 3, 0: $3 + 0 = 3, 0 + 3 = 3, 3 - 3 = 0, 3 - 0 = 3$. Charles said that we should include 0,0,0, in the list of trios!

After they had played a few rounds of the trios game they began to make trios with fractions. Andy started with $\frac{3}{4} - \frac{1}{4} = \frac{1}{2}$. Charles suggested $\frac{1}{2} - \frac{3}{4} = \frac{1}{4}$ and then changed this to $\frac{1}{2} - \frac{3}{4} = -\frac{1}{4}$. Once more I asked them to use the language patterns to match these symbolic statements. Charles said, 'Three quarters is one half more than one quarter'; Andy continued, 'One half more than one quarter is three quarters'. The children were beginning to link the concept of subtraction with fractions. We concluded with multiplication and division trios suggested by Helena, e.g. 3, 4, 12.

B. Dice games

I introduced simple dice games (addition, subtraction and multiplication of the scores on two dice) to all the groups, partly to assess the number knowledge of individual children and partly to introduce them to the concept of probability. They also made operation tables in addition (Table 1, page 23), difference (Table 2, page 24) and multiplication (Table 7, page 71) for the numbers 1 to 6. When the tables were completed I asked the children to make an ordered list of the frequencies of occurrence of each total, difference or product. They then carried out experiments with two dice and recorded their results in tabular form. Throughout I questioned the groups on a variety of topics.

(1) After the group at Missingham had found that the sum of the number pairs on opposite faces was 7, I asked them to add the numbers 1 to 6. Alec said, 'It's 3 sevens, that's 21'. 'Why seven?', I asked. Alec replied, 'The dice have six sides. If you add the numbers on the opposite sides of the die you get seven each time. There are three pairs of opposite sides so the sum is 21.'

(2) At Meakins I asked the children to tell me the greatest and least possible totals when two dice are thrown ten times and the scores are added. They all agreed that these totals must be 120 and 20. After throwing his dice, John had a total of 73. 'Is John's total more than halfway between 120 and 20?', I asked. John said, 'The halfway score is 60 – no, 50'. Chris said, 'It's 70 because half of 20 is 10, half of 120 is 60, and 10 and 60 are 70'. Some children convinced themselves that 70 was midway between 20 and 120 by drawing a number line (Figure 14).

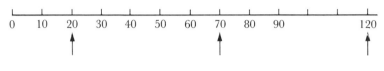

Figure 14

(3) A similar problem was discussed at Melia. After making the addition table Peter said, 'The total which occurs most often is 7'. He then looked at his experimental results which he had recorded in columns (2 to 12) on squared paper. He said, 'I think the number midway between 2 and 12 (7) has occurred most often; 6 and 8 should be next, and so on'. We compared individual results from our samples. No one had found that the total 7 occurred most frequently in their own comparatively small sample, but when we combined our results, 7 was the total which occurred most often. The children went on throwing the dice to convince themselves that with a larger sample the experimental results would resemble their theoretical table more closely.

(4) Before the group at Measures had found and tabulated the products of the scores on two dice, I asked them which products between the extremes (1 and 36) they would not be able to throw. 'Sevens and multiples of 7', Alex said; but no further suggestions were made until after they had carried out the experiment.

At Makewell, after the table of products had been made and the results of the experiment had been tabulated, I asked the group in what ways the table of products and the tabulated results were alike. Peter said, 'Both go up to 36. The numbers in the table and the numbers on the dice were the same'.

At Missingham, getting no answer, I had to rephrase the question, 'There is something the same about the multiplication table and the experiment with two dice. What did you do to the scores at each throw?' Vera said, 'Double them ... No, we multiplied them. The numbers in the table go from one to six. You can get all the numbers [products] by multiplying the scores on two dice. But we can't get odd numbers.' When she found that 22 was also an impossible product, Vera changed her mind.

(5) At Makewell I asked the children which products occurred once only in the table of products. Nora said, '1, 9, 16, 25, 36. These numbers are one times one, three times three, four times four, and so on'. None of the children in any of the groups had heard of square numbers. At Missingham, Vera noticed that the numbers on the diagonal of the product table 'differed by odd numbers'.

At Measures, Mick said, 'These numbers have differences, 3, 5, 7 .... odd numbers'. 'What number must you start with to get a difference of 1 to begin with?' I asked. Mick said, 'Zero, because the difference between one and zero is one'.

C. Sampling

In every group the sampling activities led to discussion about the two aspects of division and gave me the opportunity to introduce the appropriate language patterns. Moreover, by asking, 'How many did you have altogether?' I was able to emphasize that division and multiplication were 'reverse operations'.

I began by asking each child to take a sample of pebbles and to find out and record whether the sample was odd or even. This experiment was to be carried out ten times in all. Mick at Measures asked, 'Why can't we divide by four? – It's quicker'. I questioned him about this way of dealing with the samples. 'How will you know the evens from the odds?' I asked. Mick answered at once, 'The even samples will have no remainder or remainder two; the odds will have remainders one or three'. Mick took twenty samples while the others were taking ten. The totals were collected, collated and checked. I asked what results the children would expect. Stewart, at Missingham, who had taken ten even samples, commented, 'I see no reason why, altogether, we should have more evens than odds. Odds and evens have an equal chance.' But Nick at Movehall was not so sure. He said, 'I think there'll be more evens'. When in every group we analysed the results, the totals for odds and evens were so close that the children decided to take another set of 10 or 20 samples to see what happened. The totals remained close.

I then asked each child to take ten samples, recording for each whether the sample was a multiple of three or not. Some children pointed out that the remainders could be 1 or 2 this time, and recorded their results according to the remainders: 0, 1 or 2. They forecast that there would be more non-multiples of three because 'multiples are harder to get'.

The totals at Meakins were 22, 22 and 37. 'How do I know that these totals must be wrong?' I asked. Alec said, 'There were eight of us, so the final total should be 80, not 81'. The totals were checked and altered to 22, 22 and 36. 'Suppose the totals for each remainder had been equal, what would the totals have been?' I asked. The children found this problem difficult, perhaps because the grand total was not divisible by three, so I continued, 'Could each total have been 20?' 'No', they replied. They tried 25 next. 'That gives a grand total of 75', they said. They finally decided that 26 would give the nearest grand total to 80. (Twenty-seven would have been nearer but the children were not prepared to have a grand total of more than 80.)

I asked which total (22, 22, 36) was nearest to 26; furthest from 26. When they gave the correct answers I introduced the word average for the 'equal number'. Stewart said he had heard the word but had not known what it meant. (See M5, p. 90.)

It was interesting to notice how the methods of recording matured without any questioning from me. For example, in the odds and evens activity, the stages of development were (i) recording 'odd' or 'even' in order as these occurred; (ii) recording in columns, odd or even; (iii) recording in columns according to the remainders, e.g. 0, 1, 2, 3, when dividing samples by four; (iv) block graphs built on squared paper in columns labelled with sums, differences or products, in order.

D. The four operations

(1) *Digit sum.* The children at Melia gave quick responses to oral addition. I asked them to write the multiples of nine, in order, until they 'topped' 100; and then to add the digits for each multiple until a single figure was obtained (e.g. $99 \rightarrow 18 \rightarrow 9$). Peter volunteered, 'The tens increase by one; the units decrease by one; at 99 the digits are the same'.

M5: AVERAGES

When I asked a group of teachers what was meant by an average (rather than how they could find an average – which they all knew), an infant teacher replied, 'It's fair shares for all'. She then continued, 'All this time I've been giving my infants experience of an average without knowing it', and described the following activity.

> I offer a bag of 12 raisins to each of a group of four children. I give the fourth child all the raisins remaining in the bag. I then ask the children to show their shares (perhaps one, three, two, six). They protest, 'It isn't fair'. 'What shall we do about it then?' I ask. 'Put them all back [adding] and share them out', [dividing fairly among four] the children say. So all the raisins are returned to the bag and each child in turn takes one raisin at a time until the bag is empty. I suggest that the children check to make sure that they all have the same number of raisins. I realize now that this is an activity which will help children to acquire the concept of an average.

I discussed this activity with the group of teachers. We were full of admiration for the teacher's imagination and skill. Subsequently I applied this teacher's 'fair shares' method to other activities, without, at first, using the word 'average'. Here are two examples from one of the project schools.

(a) *Heights.*   I asked two groups of four children, one of boys and the other girls, which group would stretch farther if they were all laid out head to foot in a long line. I had provided long paper strips in different colours. The children decided to cut and label strips to match individual heights. They fastened the strips together, end to end, without overlapping the ends, then compared the two long strips. (The girls' combined strip was slightly longer than the boys'.)
'Suppose you were all the same height, what would that height be?' I asked. This prompted each group to fold the long strips (the total height of the group of four) into four equal lengths. In this way we 'acted' the concept of an average length.

(b) *Mass.*   I repeated the experiment with the same two groups. This time I asked the children to find which group had the greater total mass. I then asked, 'If in each group the mass of each child was the same, what would this mass be?' This time the children added the masses of the four children in their group and then divided the total mass by 4. At this stage I introduced the word average and began to give the children simple abstract examples, e.g. find your average score for the next ten throws of a die.

They were excited to find that the final sum of the digits of multiples of nine was always 9. They checked this by taking large multiples. Mick asked what pattern they would get for multiples of 8, 7, 6, etc. After discovering that the digit sum of successive multiples of 8 differed by 1 each time, (8, 7, 6, etc.) Peter forecast that the digit sums of multiples of 7 would have differences of 2. All the children tested each multiple in turn; they made many slips until they discovered the patterns of the digit sums for each multiple. Their work became far more accurate in consequence.

At Meakins each child started with a number fewer than 9, added 9 successively until they 'topped' 100, then found and recorded the digit sum for each number. They were thrilled to find that the digit sum was always the number they started with. Stewart put the result into words, 'The sum of the digits is always the same as the remainder when the number is divided by 9'. They tried Stewart's statement on car and telephone numbers and checked that it always worked. (See M6, p. 92.)

(2) *Subtraction.*   To provide practice in subtraction I gave activities such as the following:

(a) Start with 100; subtract nine (then eight, seven, etc.) successively until you have to stop. Record the digit sums and describe the patterns.

(b) *The 'Diffy' game.* See page 59, Figure 9.

Write *any* four whole numbers at the corners of a large diamond. Why do you have to stop? Will you eventually have to stop for any set of numbers you start with? What happens when you start with a different shape, for example, a triangle, a pentagon or a hexagon?

M6

Table 8: Digit sum of various multiples

⑦	7	⑧	8	⑨	9	⑩	1	⑪	2
14	5	16	7	18	9	20	2	22	4
21	3	24	6	27	9	30	3	33	6
28	10→1	32	5	36	9	40	4	44	8
35	8	40	4	45	9	50	5	55	10→1
42	6	48	12→3	54	9	60	6	66	12→3
49	13→4	56	11→2	63	9	70	7	77	14→5
56	11→2	64	10→1	72	9	80	8	88	16→7
63	9	72	9	81	9	90	9	99	18→9
70	7	80	8	90	9	100	1	110	2
77	14→5	88	16→7	99	18→9	110	2	121	4
84	12→3	96	15→6	108	9				

For multiples of 8, starting with 8, the digit sum decreases by 1 from 8 to 1, then starts at 9 and decreases by 1 each time ....
For multiples of 7, starting at 7, the digit sum decreases by 2 each time from 7 to 1, then starts at 8 and decreases by 2 to 2, restarts at 9 ....
I missed the opportunity of asking the children to investigate digit sums of multiples of 10, 11, etc., and to make comparisons with the digit sums of 8, 7, etc.

(c) Mental practice in examples such as 73 − 37, 92 − 29, in which the children described their methods and found the patterns of the answers.

(d) They measured their personal statistics, arranged these in order of length and found the differences between successive pairs.

When we began to discuss methods of written subtraction a teacher at Movehall said, 'I spent far too much time during the first year on written subtraction, and they cannot do it even now'. So I began with 'shopkeeper's addition', which was new to them. I asked them to make a written record of finding the change from £1 after spending 61 pence. Mick, at Measures, said that the easiest way was to subtract 1p from 40p. He then said, '61 to 91 is 30; the change is 39 pence'. Alec's method was, '61, 63, 65, 70, 80, 90, £1'. (He said he had counted up in actual coins.) We discussed how this method could be recorded and extended to 'abstract' examples such as 93 − 39.

(3) *Division.* I first had to make sure that each child could differentiate between the two aspects of division for any simple example I provided, e.g., 16 ÷ 2 as 16 divided into 2 sets (8 in each set) and as 16 divided into sets of 2 (8 sets).

The children at Melia said that they found division difficult, so I asked them to solve this problem, 'It is 90 days to Whitsun. How many weeks and days is this?' Ivor was the first to explain his mental calculation. He said, 'Ten sevens are 70, two sevens are 14, that's 84 days. So it's 12 weeks and 6 days to Whitsun.' The next problem I gave them was: 'How many coaches holding a maximum of 56 children each would be needed to take a school of 850 children on a journey?' Helena and Stephen found it difficult to record in an ordered way, and said, 'I don't get it'. The others managed to find the answer. Peter, Charles and Ivor recorded like this:

$$
\begin{array}{r}
850 \\
-\,560 \quad \text{10 coaches} \\
\hline
290 \\
-\,280 \quad \text{5 coaches} \\
\hline
10 \quad \text{1 more coach} \\
\hline
\text{16 coaches altogether}
\end{array}
$$

Most of the groups agreed that this method of long division made sense, but some of them were reluctant to change the method they had already learned and practised. Time was short and I could not spend more on division but I tried, later on, to persuade the teachers to continue with this method. Some of them did so.

(4) *Fractions* cropped up in some groups. At Melia, after a session on division, I asked: 'How many halves are there in one whole?' They all said two. I asked them to write this statement, using the division symbol. Charles wrote, $1 \div \frac{1}{2} = 2$. Ivor asked, 'Is $2 \div \frac{1}{2} = 1$?' Since this occurred during the final session I was unable to help him to see that the answer was 4. Moreover, the teachers also had difficulty with the division of fractions. At Makewell, Ted and Wong recorded: $1 \div \frac{1}{2} = \frac{4}{4}$; both boys rarely made an error of any kind. More time was needed for division situations.

M7: FRACTIONS

$1 \div \frac{1}{4}$. Division is the operation which gives the solution to the problem: How many quarters in one whole? The answer is, of course, 4. This answer can also be found by working in quarters: $1 \div \frac{1}{4} = 4 \div 1$, which is 4.

Division of fractions can always be carried out by this method (invented by an eight-year-old girl).

---

(5) *Decimals.*   I introduced decimal fractions at Measures because Hannah, the most able girl in this age group, had announced one day, 'I hate decimals from textbooks'. We began by extending the sequence:

1000 100 10 1	(which the children to described as multiply- ing by 10 moving from right to left)	$\frac{1}{10}$ $\frac{1}{100}$ $\frac{1}{1000}$

I explained the 'shorthand' method of writing these fractions (0.1, 0.01, 0.001). They arranged their personal measures in order of length, writing each in decimetres, to one decimal place. The children had no difficulty in calculating the differences between successive lengths to one decimal place.

I then asked them to draw their left footprint on square centimetre paper and to find the area in square centimetres. Hannah asked, 'What do we do about part squares?' 'What do you suggest?' I asked. 'I'll estimate part squares in fractions', was the reply. I asked them to cut a square decimetre from centimetre square paper. Some of them were surprised to discover (and others at first refused to believe) that there were one hundred centimetre squares in one square decimetre, so that one square centimetre was $\frac{1}{100}$ of a square decimetre: 0.01. We worked out one square centimetre, ten square centimetres, etc., as decimals of one square decimetre. They then expressed their foot areas as square decimetres (to two decimal places this time). I asked each of them to cut their foot area from square centimetre paper, one decimetre in width, so that, in pairs, they could compare foot areas

(Figure 15). Hannah announced, 'My foot area is 0.02 square decimetres larger than Ann's'. I regretted that we were unable to return to this topic, but I was glad that all the children in this group clearly understood what they were doing and enjoyed the activities.

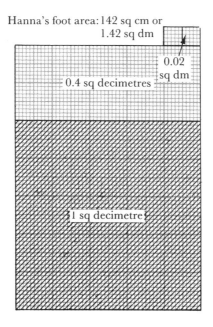

Hanna's foot area: 142 sq cm or 1.42 sq dm

0.02 sq dm

0.4 sq decimetres

1 sq decimetre

Figure 15

E. Multiples and prime numbers

I found that nearly all the children were uncertain about multiplication facts, even multiples of three. I therefore decided to introduce prime numbers and thereby to focus attention systematically on multiples and factors. I knew that none of the children had heard about prime numbers before.

I provided identical plastic squares and asked the children, in pairs, to make as many different rectangles (including squares) as they could for each number in turn. Most of the groups went as far as 20. Figure 16 shows the beginning of the sequence.

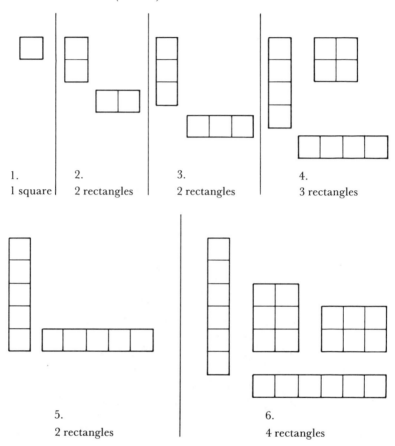

Figure 16

When I asked the children what they noticed about the sequence, they said that there was one square on its own, and that up to 13 half the numbers were two-rectangle numbers. I explained that these two-rectangle numbers were called primes and that we were going to concentrate on prime numbers. I asked, 'Why do prime numbers have two rectangles only?' 'Because they have no other multiples', was the reply.

At the next session I asked the children in all the groups to make a six-day calendar (Table 9) as far as 60 days, and to mark all the prime numbers. As Mick, at Measures, made his table he commented, 'The numbers in each column have a difference of six'. All the children in this group, even Hannah, marked several multiples of 3 as primes. At Movehall, where we had not yet found the digit-sum of multiples of 3, most of these multiples were first marked as primes. In every group we then took time to find the characteristics of various multiples. Once the 3, 6, 9, pattern of the digit-sum of multiples of 3 was appreciated, there were no more mistakes. One of the multiples which intrigued the children was the pattern of multiples of 11 greater than 100. (110, 121, 132, 143, 154 ....) They found the pattern difficult to describe. Nora, at Makewell, first suggested, 'The difference between the first two digits gives the third digit'. I asked her if she could describe the pattern in another way. Finally she said, 'The first and third digits add to the digit in the middle'.

Table 9: Six-day calendar

1	(2)	(3)	4	(5)	6
(7)	8	9	10	(11)	12
(13)	14	15	16	(17)	18
(19)	20	21	22	(23)	24
25	26	27	28	(29)	30
(31)	32	33	34	35	36
(37)	38	39	40	(41)	42

When the six-day calendar was completed correctly (Table 9) I asked the children to describe the positions of the prime numbers in the table. Charles, at Melia, gave the most comprehensive description, 'After the first row the primes are in the first and fifth columns. But there are numbers in these columns which aren't primes. These are 25, 49, 55, 35 .... These are multiples of 5, or of 7, or of both.' He then continued his calendar to 100 days to check that his suggestion was correct.

At Missingham, to provide further practice in spotting multiples, I collected house numbers from the group. Joanne lived at number 695. 'What can you say about this number?' I asked. Joanne said, 'It's divisible by 5. The other factor is 139.' They tried their knowledge of multiples of 3 and 11 and decided that 139 was prime. I asked each child to bring five car numbers to the next session. I asked them how we could sort the collection. Valerie suggested sorting into odd and even numbers. Andy said, 'Let's collect multiples of 5'. Stewart said, 'Let's make a collection of all the digits in order'. He did this and recorded the frequency with which each digit occurred. I asked him if he thought that the number of digits in each set would be the same if the collection was large enough. After a pause, Stewart said, 'No, because car numbers don't begin with 0'.

We revised the characteristics of other multiples. 'How can you tell multiples of 4?', I asked. They hesitated. 'Is 100 divisible by 4?' I asked. 'Yes', they said. 'Is 500 divisible by 4?' I continued. 'No – yes, it is', they said. When they had decided that multiples of 4 could be detected by finding whether the last two digits were multiples of 4 we turned our attention to multiples of 8.

I gave all the groups quick practice in multiples, using sets of cards numbered 0 to 16, arranged in a line in number order.

I asked them to move the set of odd numbers up and to describe the pattern of the cards in this set. 'Alternates', they said. 'What is the pattern of the cards in the lower row?' I asked. 'Alternates, except at the beginning', was the reply. (Some of them had pushed zero half way up.) 'Does this suggest anything about zero?' I asked. 'Is zero odd or even?' (Figure 17).

At Melia, Charles said, 'Zero ought to be neutral'. Peter said, 'Zero belongs to both sets'. I asked them to count down in twos first from 11, and then from 12. They were still reluctant to concede that zero belonged to the set of even numbers. I asked them to put their cards in order in one line again and to push up the multiples of 3. Once again they were reluctant to include zero as a multiple of 3, though they found the pattern more compelling this time. We discussed the multiples of 3, in order, ending with zero once the pattern was established. Later on, when the children were familiar with square and cube numbers, I included these numbers in the sequences we made with the numbered cards.

I reinforced the work on multiples by asking the children to put cards numbered 1 to 16 (as the universal set) on a sheet of paper. They used wool loops of different colours to sort the cards into sets: a blue loop to contain the multiples of 2; a red loop to contain the square numbers (later on, a green loop to contain the multiples of 3, etc.). As loops were added I asked the children to describe each region. For example, when the red and blue loops were in position the children described the regions as: square numbers which were multiples of 2;

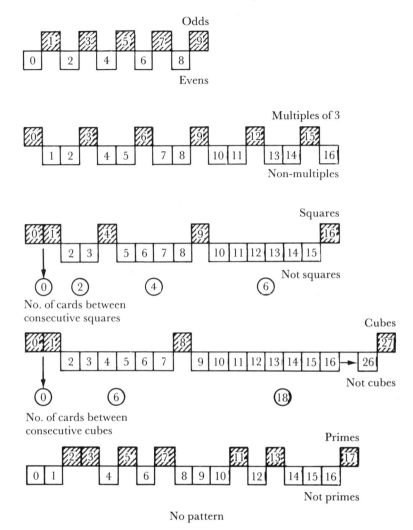

Figure 17: Number patterns

square numbers which were not multiples of 2; numbers which were multiples of 2 but not squares, and numbers which were not squares and not multiples of 2. At this stage all the children included zero in the multiples. When they discussed the prime numbers zero was eventually described as 'the perfect multiple'. (See Figure 18.)

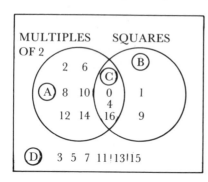

Region

A: Multiples of 2 which are not squares.

B: Squares which are not multiples of 2 ('odd' squares).

C: Square numbers which are multiples of 2 ('even' squares).

D: Numbers which are neither square nor multiples of 2.

Figure 18

F. Scale: squares and cubes

(1) *Squares.*   We began by using identical squares of two colours to build larger squares. In the course of the activities all the children discovered the odd number pattern of the differences between successive squares. All of them included zero (without protest) at the beginning of the sequence of squares, in order to complete the odd number pattern of differences within the sequence (Table 10). Florence, at Missingham, said, 'If a square hasn't got an edge then it hasn't got an area either', when we were discussing what a zero square really meant. Some of the children made squares using two colours alternately (Figure 19). 'Did you use the same number of each colour?', I asked. At Meakins, Stewart said, 'For odd squares the number of squares of each colour differs by one'. 'What do you mean by an "odd" square?', I asked. Walter answered, 'Odd squares have an odd number of units in each edge. The areas are odd too. Even squares have even areas.' At Movehall, Rowena gave a more accurate description, 'The number of units of the two colours differs by one in squares with an odd number of units in the edges'. (At the end of this session Rowena said, 'I prefer written sums to finding patterns using squares'.)

Table 10

Square numbers		0	1	4	9	16	25	36
Difference pattern			1	3	5	7	9	11

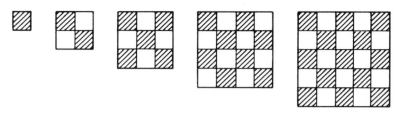

Figure 19: Squares made using units of alternate colours

Some of the children used the two colours for successive layers as they made sequences of enlarging squares. At Meakins, Walter started with a square at one corner, built round two edges of the corner square (Figure 20) and, once more, noticed the odd number pattern. Peter started with one square in the middle, built all round this square and described his layer pattern: 1, 8, 16, 24 .... He described his successive squares as 'the odd squares'. John started with four squares in the middle and built round this 2 by 2 square. He said, 'I've made the even squares. The pattern of the layers is: 4, 12, 20, 28 ....'

I next provided unit squares of one colour, and asked the children to take two handfuls each and, without counting, to make the largest square frame they could. When they had finished, I asked each child to say what the edge of the square was and how many units had been used altogether. At first every child multiplied the number of units in the edge by 4 to obtain the total. At Movehall, David was the first to say, 'I've counted the corners twice. I made a frame of edge 10 units. Multiply the number of units by 4, then subtract 4. I used $40 - 4$, 36 units.'

At Missingham, the children discussed the sequence of frames. Vera asked, 'Is a two by two square really a frame with no hole in the middle?' All the children in this group decided to include this square as the smallest in the sequence of frames. I asked them to describe the sequence of holes in the frames. Stewart said, 'The holes make the squares 1, 4, 9, 16'. (He had omitted the zero hole.) Vera then noticed that she had counted the corners twice when she found the number of units she had used for her 10 by 10 frame. Andy said, 'Then you should take away the corners first, that leaves eight on each side; multiply by 4, then put 4 back: $32 + 4 = 36$'.

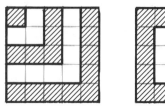 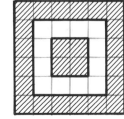

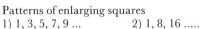

Patterns of enlarging squares
1) 1, 3, 5, 7, 9 ...   2) 1, 8, 16 .....   3) 4, 12, 20 ....

Figure 20

At Makewell, for his 6 by 6 frame, David said he found twice 6 and twice 4 and added to find the number of units he had used. Hilda had a different method, 'I made a 6 by 6 frame. I took 1 from 6, that's 5, and multiplied this by 4 to find the number of units I used, 20.' (See Fig. 13, p. 80.) The children then made sequences of square frames and their holes:

Frames   6 by 6   5 by 5   4 by 4   3 by 3   2 by 2

Holes   4 by 4   3 by 3   2 by 2   1 by 1   zero hole

When I asked if this suggested another way of finding the number of units they had used, Wong said, 'Subtract the number of units in the square hole from the number of units in the large square (Figure 21). For the 3 by 3 frame subtract 1 from 9, which is 8.'

(2) *Three-dimensional enlargement.*   I provided identical interlocking cubes and asked the children to make a larger scale model of a 2-cube or 3-cube model. They all began with a model in which they doubled the dimensions but in their first attempts, not surprisingly, two dimensions only were doubled. Some of them did not progress beyond completing the doubling model. I asked them to find the ratio of the volume of the larger model to that of the smaller one. They found this to be eight and obtained the same ratio when I gave them the easier activity of building enlarging cubes. Ivor, at Melia, not only completed a model in which the dimensions were tripled (he used 81 cubes) but found the ratio of the volumes to be 27 to 1, and found the same ratio when he made a 'triple' cube.

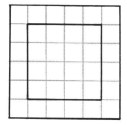

Wong's method for finding the number of units
used for the frame 36 – 16

**Figure 21: Finding the frame by subtracting inner square from
outer square**

To emphasize the consequences of the large increase in volume
(and therefore of weights) as young animals grew into adults, I gave
the children at Melia the following problem. 'When a young elephant
grows so that its dimensions are doubled, what happens to its weight?'
The children told me that its weight would then be eight times its
birth weight. I continued, 'If the dimensions of the elephant's feet are
doubled, would its feet be able to support its increased weight?' I gave
them squared paper so that the children could draw an enlargement
of an elephant's foot. Ivor said, 'Let's pretend that the foot is square,
it's easier'. When they drew the enlarged foot they decided that if the
dimensions were doubled the feet could support only 4 times the birth
weight. 'What should the dimensions be to support 8 times the birth
weight?' I asked. Ivor drew a square with its dimensions tripled and
answered, 'The foot dimensions must be multiplied by 3 because the
foot area is then 9 times what it was to begin with' (Figure 22).

At Makewell the children had enough cubes to complete a sequence
as far as 4 by 4 by 4. I asked them to continue to a 6 by 6 by 6 cube.
They had trouble in working out the volume of the '6' cube. I asked
them to make a table of all the facts they had discovered about cubes
and squares. After some discussion they decided to include base
perimeter, base area and volume. I suggested that they should include
total 'skin' area because I wanted to see if they could appreciate the
rate at which the number of squares of skin for each cube changed
with enlargement. They managed this for the first three enlarging

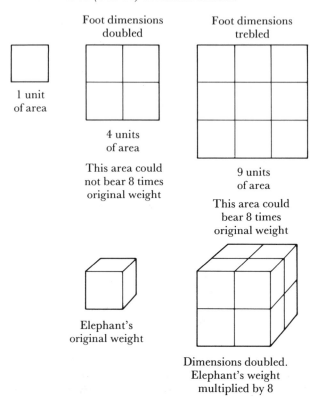

Figure 22: Elephant's foot area

cubes with the models in front of them, and then the calculations defeated them. Moreover, they needed far more experience to acquire the concept.

G. Containers – their shapes, volumes and cross-sections

I wanted to find the extent of the children's understanding of volume and surface (skin) area. I provided a water bottle with an elliptical cross-section and a yoghurt pot of circular section with the same perimeters at their widest sections; two rocks of different shape but about the same volume, and some water in a clear container. The work developed differently in each group.

In some groups I began by asking the children how they could find out how much space they took up themselves, introducing the word volume for this concept. At Makewell, Hilda suggested, 'You could lie down and get someone to draw round you'. 'Would that really tell you how much space you took up?', I asked. I showed the children the two rocks. 'Which is larger? How could we find out?' 'Weigh them – no, grind them to powder and compare the amounts', said George. We had nothing suitable to grind them with, so I asked the children if they could use the container of water to compare the volumes of the rocks. 'Compare the water levels when you put each one into the water separately', Una said. They did this and found how close the rocks were in volume.

We returned to a discussion of how the children might discover their own volumes. Peter suggested, 'We could stand in a bath – but a swimming bath would be too big'. 'Why?', I asked. 'You would not notice the water going up', was the reply. David took over, 'In the bath at home you need to fill it up to cover all of you with water'. Ernest continued, 'Put in about five inches of water. Get in. The water will come to about 13 inches. Measure how far the water has gone up.' At this point the children had to go to another lesson. At the next session a week later we returned to the topic. Ernest started again. 'Fill the bath to 12 inches.' (Later on, Ernest corrected this height to 30 centimetres but left the others in inches.) 'Step in to be covered with water. The level might go up to 13 inches. Measure the rise. Let the water out, then put an inch in again.' 'How could you measure this quantity of water?', I asked. Unfortunately I had let slip the word litre the week before. The children had no idea what this unit looked like, but they noticed that my water bottle was labelled 1.13 litres. Peter said, 'We could count the number of litre bottles needed to fill the bath to one inch'.

At Melia, when discussing how to find his own volume, Charles first suggested making a mould to fit his body, then counting the number of litres of water required to fill the mould. He then suggested that the bath too should be completely filled with water. 'Get in and measure the displacement', he finished. This was rejected as too messy. 'Suppose you do not fill the tub to the brim', I said, 'but only partly fill it, what would you have to do?' Helena said, 'The water would rise. Measure the flat area [of the bath] and how much the water rises.' Andy interrupted, 'You need someone else to make a mark – no, two marks. Then measure that amount of water.' I asked

Charles (who had said that water is measured in litres) how many litres he thought his volume might be. 'Four or five', he said, looking at my water bottle. I told the children that my displacement was about 50 litres but they were not ready to estimate their own.

We then began to investigate the water bottle and the yoghurt pot when each was filled to the brim with water. 'Can you pick the two containers up without spilling the water?' I asked. At Meakins, Peter tried to pick the yoghurt pot up. He exclaimed, 'I can't pick it up without spilling some water because it's heavy'. 'What do you mean by heavy?', I asked. 'About one pound', was the answer. So Sarah tried to pick up the yoghurt pot. This time the children heard the water overflow. So she tried the water bottle. She pressed the short sides but the water did not come out (Figure 23). 'Why does the water overflow from the pot but not from the bottle?' I asked. Sarah answered, 'Because the bottle is strong. The water [level] went down, not up.' I suggested that she should try to pick the bottle up the other way, pressing the longer sides. Sarah found that this time the water overflowed. This led to a discussion about new tubes of toothpaste which the children said were circular at the top. They agreed that the tube had to be pressed to get the toothpaste out. Rajah said that the shape of the bottle must have something to do with the way the water behaved, overflowing when pressed one way, going down when pressed the other way. I asked the children how they could find out which was larger, the ellipse of the bottle or the circle of the yoghurt pot. Walter said, 'Put the water in a jug'. I pointed out that this time it was area we wanted to measure, not volume. 'Get paper and cut out the cross section', suggested Alec. While we were wondering how to do this, Alec decided that the first thing to do was to compare the perimeters of the pot and the bottle at their widest. They were surprised to find that both perimeters were 28 centimetres. This made them more determined than ever to find the areas of the two cross sections. This took time, because the largest section of the bottle was part way up. Eventually the sections were traced on squared paper. The area of the circle was found to be 70 square centimetres and that of the ellipse 50 square centimetres. The children at Melia found that they could press the bottle until it was almost circular in shape. 'It will hold more now', Charles said. 'Why don't manufacturers make more cylinders?'

In all the groups we continued with this topic. I asked the children to find the shape and the area of the largest rectangle with perimeter

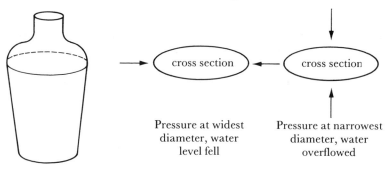

Figure 23

28 centimetres. Some of them thought that the largest rectangle might be a square because the circle was larger in area than the ellipse. 'Give me the dimensions of some of the rectangles', I said. '13 by 1, 12 by 2, 11 by 3 ....' were suggested. I asked them to make an ordered list of the rectangles (Table 11) and then, working in pairs, to cut out the complete set of rectangles (reversals included), to label each with its area, and to arrange the set in some kind of order.

Table 11: Rectangles with perimeter 20 cm only

	Width cm	Length cm	Area sq cm
	0	10	0
	1	9	9
	2	8	16
	3	7	21
	4	6	24
largest area	5	5	25
	6	4	24
	7	3	21
	8	2	16
	9	1	9
	10	0	0

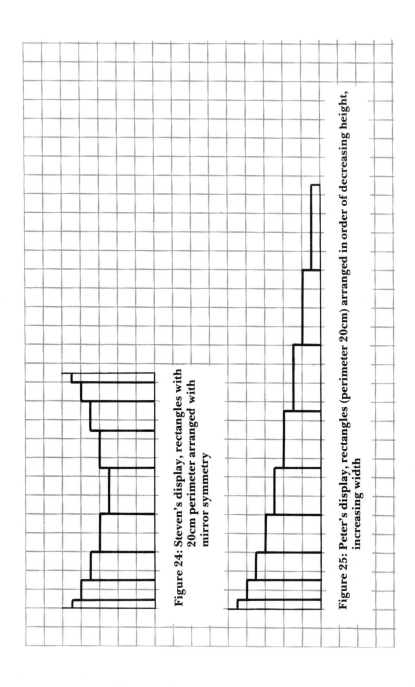

Figure 24: Steven's display, rectangles with 20cm perimeter arranged with mirror symmetry

Figure 25: Peter's display, rectangles (perimeter 20cm) arranged in order of decreasing height, increasing width

At Melia, I asked the pairs of children how they had decided about the arrangement of the rectangles. Steven said, 'We made the heights decrease and then increase to make a symmetrical pattern' (Figure 24). Peter said, 'We put them in order of height: highest, then second highest and so on'. 'What is happening to the widths?' I asked. 'Getting bigger', Andy answered (Figure 25). I asked them which rectangle had the smallest area. 'The one with the longest height', Charles answered. 'Could you find an even smaller area than any here?', I asked. The children decided that the rectangle would have to be longer still: '13½ cm by ½ cm, that's 6¾ square centimetres area', was the first suggestion. '13¾ cm by ¼ cm, 13.9 cm by 0.1 cm', they continued. At this point Charles said, 'You could squash out all the area if you wanted to'.

At Makewell, Hilda was not sure that the square had the largest area. She decided to make a regular triangle. Her group had made sets of rectangles with perimeter 20 centimetres. 'What length will you make the edges of your triangle?' I asked. Hilda said 6 centimetres, but David said that the edges should be 6½ centimetres, which would give a perimeter of 19½ centimetres. Hilda tried both 6½ cm and 7 cm for the edges but found that all these triangles had a smaller area than 25 square centimetres, the area of a square with perimeter 20 centimetres.

It was interesting to find that this problem, which started from the investigation of two containers of different shapes, developed in so many ways.

III. Findings from these sessions

1. The children in these groups rarely tired of the problems I gave them, however late in the day the session took place. They responded enthusiastically and enjoyed being made to think and to use their imagination. They never ran out of ideas and were willing to try anything.

2. Frequently these children developed problems further without any prompting from me.

3. The methods they used to record the results of their experiments gradually became more sophisticated.

4. No one ever queried the need to use materials to solve problems.

5. They soon became confident in their ability to solve problems. It never occurred to any of them that they might not be able to handle

any problem I set them. But they found some mental calculations difficult (since they had so little practice in these at school) and resorted to paper and pencil, for example, when completing the skin area/volume section in the table of squares and cubes.

6. For my part, I found these age groups as a whole the most rewarding of all. At the end all except two children said that they had enjoyed everything they had done, and asked, 'Who will take us when you go?'

Activities used with children of ages 8 to 10

Slow learners	*Able children*
1. Estimating, organizing and checking number of objects in a collection p.21	1. Number trios pp. 85–86
2. Sampling: odds and evens pp. 21–22	2. Odds and evens, remainders from multiples of 3; averages p. 88–89
3. Two-dice games: addition and difference; tables for set of numbers 1 to 6. pp. 22–24	3. Two-dice games: addition, difference and products; frequencies analysed from tables for pairs of numbers 1 to 6 p. 86–87
4. Place value: 2-digit numbers; HTU dice game; card game pp. 24–25 Build and break a cube (multi-base blocks) p. 25 Using number lines pp. 25–26	

Slow learners	*Able children*
5. Four operations: addition p.26	5. Continuous addition of 9, digit
subtraction (shopkeeper's	sum, p. 89, p. 92
addition) pp. 28–29	Subtraction p. 91
multiplication (adding	Multiples and prime numbers
equal sets) pp. 29–32	pp. 95–100
division situations p. 32	Scale: sequence of enlarging
Sequence of square numbers	squares p.100–103
p. 34	Scale: 3D enlargement;
	sequence of cubes pp. 102–104

6. Fractions and decimals:
   pp. 93–95

7. Capacities of containers of
   different cross-sections p. 104–
   107
   Variation in the areas of
   rectangles with the same
   perimeter p. 107–109

Activities used with able third and fourth years at middle schools and some of their responses

I. Introduction

The pupils in these older groups faced difficulties which had not arisen with the younger ones. First, there was a greater difference in the extent of the mathematical knowledge possessed by the third and the fourth years than in that possessed by the first and the second years. The third years were acutely conscious of this difference and it was some time before they gained sufficient confidence to take an active part in oral work and discussion. This was particularly true of the girls, who were often outnumbered by the boys; they needed much encouragement to make their contributions. Occasionally they failed to understand a suggestion made by a fourth year and it was some time before they were willing to say so.

Secondly, in all the schools the heads and the teachers said that the fourth years became increasingly unsettled (and sometimes unco-operative) in anticipation of their transfer to a high school. In the spring term (the first term of my work with these children) many of them were anxious about their choice of school. Some were taking entrance examinations for independent schools; all were making a choice of high school. In the summer term they were waiting to hear the decision about their future schools and anticipating the problems that might arise. Moreover, in the middle school they were seniors with responsibility; at the high school they would be very junior. A television programme featuring a specific high school in the locality had increased the anxiety felt by many children.

School journeys were another unsettling influence in the summer term. During the third and fourth years these usually lasted a week and therefore some children were absent for a session. Furthermore, although the children undoubtedly derived a great deal from these journeys, they often returned to school exhausted by travelling (sometimes overseas). During the week that followed they found it hard to concentrate on mathematics, particularly on afternoons when they had already had mathematics in the morning.

In none of the project schools was the mathematics coordinator giving special attention to any of the able children on a regular basis. Most of them were given textbooks from which they had to work on their own, or with another pupil. Although they were told to ask for help when necessary, they confessed that they rarely did so. They were unaccustomed to working in a group and therefore to peer group discussion. Most of them had positive attitudes to mathematics, perhaps because they rarely came across problems they were unable to solve. Within the textbooks, the problems they met always followed a series of calculations to which these were immediately related – so they never had to decide what the situation was and which operation was needed. They were rarely, if ever, asked to undertake sustained investigations which required intensive thought.

But these fourth year children suffered another deprivation because they so frequently worked from textbooks on their own. They were accustomed to writing their solutions and calculations and missed the opportunities given to the rest of the fourth years for regular mental calculations. In consequence they made many slips when carrying out calculations in their heads. For example, they could not simplify fractions such as $\frac{32}{64}$ and so failed to recognize that there was a number pattern.

II. Content

A. Introduction

With the older groups in the middle schools I had to be particularly careful to keep the mathematical content within the capacity of primary teachers who had had no special course in mathematics, so that they could develop or replicate it. (Today an increasing number of coordinators for mathematics are attending LEA courses or Diploma courses offered by the Mathematical Association to increase their background knowledge of the subject.)

The groups responded very differently to the problems I provided. Some of the children were surprised to be given problems for which they had to use material – for example, cubes. They thought these were only for slow or young children. A few of them (at Movehall and Missingham) were angry that they seemed to be expected to use material of any kind. (Of course I assured them that they could work the problems in their imagination if they preferred to do so. Did their lack of experience with material make them feel insecure?)

By contrast, the children at Melia, Makewell and Measures were most appreciative of problems centred on real objects. At Measures, the children always began to use the material immediately without waiting to be given the problem! They created and solved their own problems. These three groups were extremely lively and imaginative at any time of day. A few of the other children were unwilling to work with their peers and much preferred to work on their own. These children usually maintained that they preferred working problems from textbooks to exchanging ideas with their peers. I tried to provide experiences of both kinds.

Although I had an overall plan the sessions with different groups developed in different ways, depending on the group or individual responses. The content included the following topics:

1. Sampling: occurrence of multiples of 2, 3 and 4, recorded according to remainders.
2. Dice games: operations using the scores on two dice; comparison with operation tables for the numbers 1 to 6.
3. Decimal fractions as an extension of place value; operations on decimals. Multiplication of fractions. (These were topics the children said they found difficult.)
4. Long division by a whole number, using the subtraction of multiples of 100, 10, etc.
5. Properties of multiples of 3, 9, 11, found by adding the digits of the multiples.
6. Prime numbers.
7. Scale: three-dimensional and two-dimensional models. Sequences, and the patterns of squares and cubes. Number patterns of perimeters, squares and cubes. The number of squares showing per cube on scale models of different sizes. Ratio and rate.
8. Containers: properties of their material. Volume and capacity and the units in which they are measured. An investigation into the areas of cross-sections with the same perimeter. Shapes with the same area; an investigation into their perimeters.

9. Graphical representation. Graphs associated with multiplication tables; perimeters, squares and cubes; inverse relationships and their graphs. Generalization and limits.

The order in which these topics were covered varied considerably from group to group. There were two reasons for this. The first was that since I had assumed that older able children would have a good knowledge of number facts, and of the processes of the four operations, I did not include these topics in the programme. However, when points of confusion about number concepts became evident within the groups, I dealt with these points immediately. The second reason was that these older children took me up on my offer not only to deal with any suggestions they made during our investigations but also to follow up any problem in which they were particularly interested.

B. The progress of the sessions

(1) *Sampling*   Surprisingly, some of the children in this age group thought that, in the final count, there should be more of one remainder than another. For example, Sheila, at Meakins, when taking samples and dividing by 3, said, 'I think there'll be more samples with remainder 2 than 1 because 2 is near 3'. After carrying out the experiment, she changed her mind. Yet Norah and Santos at Movehall decided at once that, 'There will be more non-multiples of 3 because each remainder has only a one to three chance. Multiples of 3 should be only one third of the total.' At Measures Matthew said, 'We should have one third multiples of three this time because there are three chances, [remainder] 2, 1 and 0.'

When I asked the groups what the sub-totals would be if the number of evens and odds had been equal, they gave the answer immediately (and also for the average when dividing by 3 and by 4). The children at Measures were intrigued by the fact that 'the numbers of odds and of evens are the same "distance" from the average'. They tried a second set of samples to see whether their first result was a freak. Then Matthew said, 'The chance for odd and even samples is 50%, so odds and evens will always be the same number from the half total'.

(2) *Dice activities*   The groups enjoyed recording the results of using different operations on the scores obtained by throwing a pair

of dice. They had no difficulty in analysing operation tables for the numbers 1 to 6, nor in relating these tables to the experimental results. They gave precise descriptions of the number patterns on the diagonals.

Another group of 10 and 11-year-olds played, in pairs, a version of 'Shut the box', a game from the Isle of Man. Each had a pack of cards from 0 to 12, which they spread out in number order face up on the table, and two dice. At each throw both children were allowed to perform any or all of the four operations on the two dice scores. For each result the matching card could be turned face down. For example, when the dice scores are 2 and 6 the following cards can be turned over: 8 (6 + 2), 4 (6 − 2), 12 (6 × 2), 3 (6 ÷ 2). A card could be turned down once only. The first to have all his cards turned down was the winner. I then asked the children to make the four operation tables for the numbers 1 to 6 (Table 1, page 23; Table 2, page 24; Table 7, page 71; Table 13, page 119). They analysed these tables to find the frequency of occurrence, in all four tables, of each of the numbers 0 to 12. Jenny, who collated this work, found the frequencies to be as in Table 12. She discussed her discoveries with the group.

Table 12: Frequency of occurrence of each of the scores 0 to 12 in addition, difference, multiplication and division tables

	0	1	2	3	4	5	6	7	8	9	10	11	12
Addition Table (1)	0	0	1	2	3	4	5	6	5	4	3	2	1
Difference Table (2)	6	10	8	6	4	2							
Multiplication Table (7)	0	1	2	2	3	2	4	0	2	1	2	0	4
Division Table (13)	0	6	3	2	1	1	1						
Total	6	17	14	12	11	9	10	6	7	5	5	2	5 (109)

1 occurred most often; 11 least often.

(3) *Decimal and vulgar fractions*

(a) Decimals. All the children understood how decimals fitted into the place value sequence: $\dfrac{1000 \quad 100 \quad 10 \quad 1 \quad \frac{1}{10} \quad \frac{1}{100}}{\div 10} \rightarrow$ At first, the children at Measures described this pattern as 'taking away nine'. Then they changed their description to 'dividing by 10'. I decided to give them problems on the application of decimal fractions to their own measures. I asked them to measure and record the perimeters of their head, face, neck, foot, etc., first in centimetres, then in decimetres. Using decimetres, and working to one place of decimals, they found the difference between pairs of measures, the average within the group for each measure, and the ratio of waist to neck measure (using a calculator).

We used square decimetres cut from square centimetre paper to give practice in working to two decimal places. For example, I asked the children at Measures to use a square decimetre to find the difference between 0.16 and 0.3 (Figure 26). (At first they all said that 0.16 was larger than 0.3. I gave them plenty of practice until they were quick and accurate.)

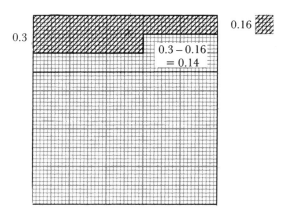

Figure 26

I then asked them to find the area of their left foot. To my surprise this was the first time any of the children had been asked to find the area of an irregular shape. A few of them neglected the part squares altogether (Robert and Daniel at Melia)! I then asked them to cut from square centimetre paper an area equivalent to their foot area, one decimetre wide. They now recorded foot area in square decimetres and, in pairs, compared foot areas and checked this by matching the new cut-outs. They also found the average foot area for the group, both from the cut-outs and by calculation.

Finally, I asked the groups to calculate their approximate skin area, using the St. John's Ambulance Association's approximation; the foot area is 1% of the body area (used also by burns units). The children were interested but they took some time to sort out realistic area units. Alec, at Missingham, declared that his skin area was 175 square metres! We compared his true skin area with the area of the room. Donald at Missingham found his skin area to be 1.6 square metres. I asked all the children to cut the skin area of the smallest of the group from newspaper and to try it 'for good fit'. Donald first cut a square of newspaper of edge 1.6 metres. He looked at this and then realized that this square had an area of more than 2½ square metres. He reduced the model to 1.6 metres by 1 metre and found that this 'was quite a good fit' (Figure 27).

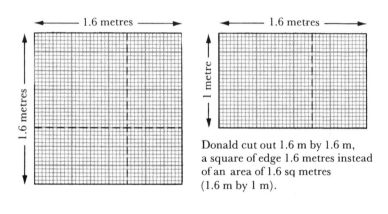

Donald cut out 1.6 m by 1.6 m,
a square of edge 1.6 metres instead
of an area of 1.6 sq metres
(1.6 m by 1 m).

Figure 27

(b) Multiplication and division of fractions. At Makewell I asked the group to include division among the operation tables they made for pairs of numbers from the set one to six. I suggested that they should leave the results as fractions so that the patterns could be seen more easily. (See Table 13.) Hazel, who had been absent, asked what 2 ÷ 2 really meant. Steve said, 'It means "How many twos in 2?"'. 'So what does 3 ÷ 2 mean?', Hazel asked. Steve replied, 'It means how many twos in 3, and that's one and a half'. Hazel persisted with her questions, 'What is 1 ÷ 2? Is it 1 or 2?' This made me realize that these children were confused about the two aspects of division. No one offered the alternative interpretation: 'What is one half of 2 or 3?' So we discussed the two aspects of division applied to whole numbers (for example, 12 divided into 3 equal sets and 12 divided into sets of 3) before applying division to fractions.

Table 13: Division of numbers 1 to 6

6	6	$\frac{6}{2}$	$\frac{6}{3}$	$\frac{6}{4}$	$\frac{6}{5}$	1
5	5	$\frac{5}{2}$	$\frac{5}{3}$	$\frac{5}{4}$	1	$\frac{5}{6}$
4	4	$\frac{4}{2}$	$\frac{4}{3}$	1	$\frac{4}{5}$	$\frac{4}{6}$
3	3	$\frac{3}{2}$	1	$\frac{3}{4}$	$\frac{3}{5}$	$\frac{3}{6}$
2	2	1	$\frac{2}{3}$	$\frac{2}{4}$	$\frac{2}{5}$	$\frac{2}{6}$
1	1	$\frac{1}{2}$	$\frac{1}{3}$	$\frac{1}{4}$	$\frac{1}{5}$	$\frac{1}{6}$
÷	1	2	3	4	5	6

At Missingham another problem arose. While we were discussing the table of squares and cubes Edwin said, 'Multiplication always means an increase'. Some of the others also held this erroneous idea. I gave them all squared paper and asked if Edwin's statement also applied when one number (or both) was a fraction. I asked them to find the area of a square with edge $\frac{1}{2}$ centimetre. They looked puzzled. 'What does area mean?' I asked. Alice answered, 'The space it takes up'. 'What does "space it takes up" really mean?', I asked. Alice then said, 'Area is the extent of a surface'. Before she had used the squared paper she said, '$\frac{1}{2} \times \frac{1}{2}$ must be $\frac{3}{4}$'. Mary said, 'No, it's 1'. They then drew Figure 28 and Alice changed her mind. She said, 'The area of the small square is $\frac{1}{4}$ of a square centimetre', and showed the diagram she had drawn. Her diagram showed clearly that $\frac{1}{4}$ was smaller than $\frac{1}{2}$. Edwin then agreed, 'So multiplication doesn't always cause an increase'. Mary suggested another way of finding $\frac{1}{2} \times \frac{1}{2}$. 'Find half a length, then halve it again and you get a quarter.' I told the group that Mary had really shown that half of a half was also a quarter.

All the children found multiplying fractions difficult unless they drew a diagram on squared paper. Raoul at Meakins had found 18×14 by adding 18×10 and 18×4 and had checked by a diagram (Figure 29). But he could not apply this method to $1\frac{1}{4} \times 1\frac{1}{4}$ ($1\frac{1}{4} \times 1 + 1\frac{1}{4} \times \frac{1}{4}$).

Figure 28

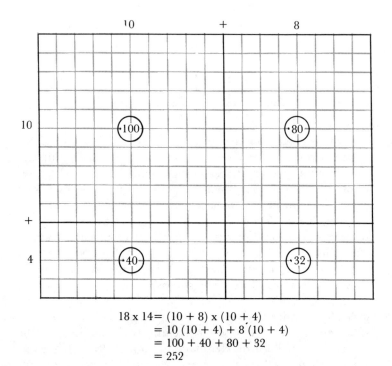

$$18 \times 14 = (10 + 8) \times (10 + 4)$$
$$= 10 (10 + 4) + 8 (10 + 4)$$
$$= 100 + 40 + 80 + 32$$
$$= 252$$

Figure 29: Long multiplication

(4) *Long division by a whole number*   Robert, at Melia, in his effort to find the ratio of 81 to 3, said, '30 is 10 threes, 60 is 20 threes; 21 left from 81; 21 is 7 threes; that's 27 threes altogether. So the ratio is 27 to 1.' I explained that Robert had invented a new method of division. I then gave them practice in recording this method, e.g. for 729 ÷ 49. They recorded:

$$
\begin{array}{rl}
729 & \\
-\,490 & 10 \times 49 \\
\hline
239 & \\
196 & 4 \times 49 \\
\hline
43 & 14 \times 49 \quad \text{14 and 43 over.} \\
\end{array}
$$

I asked if they could write the remainder in any other way. Steve suggested $\frac{43}{49}$, which he said must be less than 1 because $\frac{43}{49}$ was less than $\frac{49}{49}$.

At the beginning of the next session I asked the group to find out how many weeks and days it was to the end of term, 100 days later. To my surprise everyone used the traditional method of long division, 'slaughtering' figures for every subtraction. When I questioned the method (after our discussion of Robert's new method last session) Daniel said, 'Teachers expect this method, you know'. I asked if they remembered Robert's method of long division. Steve said, 'Subtract ten times the number'. They recorded the new example by this method. Peter then said, 'Let's do a harder example: 1719 ÷ 11.' Nora began by subtracting 100 × 11. She then suggested subtracting 10 × 11. 'Can you suggest a larger multiple?' I asked. Daniel said 220, Nora 330, Steve 440 and Peter 550. They then recorded:

$$
\begin{array}{rl}
1719 & \\
-\,1100 & 100 \times 11 \\
\hline
619 & \\
-\,550 & 50 \times 11 \\
\hline
69 & \\
-\,66 & 6 \times 11 \\
\hline
3 & 156 \times 11 \quad \text{156, 3 over.} \\
\end{array}
$$

The fourth years invented and recorded even harder divisions, but the third years continued with simpler examples. They had not previously learned long division.

(5) *Multiples: the pattern of digit sums*   I asked the children within each group to start with any number fewer than 10, to add 9 repeatedly until they topped 100, and then to add the digits until they obtained a single digit. The children were totally unprepared for the results (Table 14). I reinforced the discovery in some groups by ask-

ing the children to make a collection of car and of telephone numbers and to find out which of these numbers were divisible by 9. When there was a remainder I asked the children to record the remainder. They all added digits to test for divisibility by 9 and checked by division. In every group there was one child at least who asked, 'Would you get the same remainder if you divided by 8?', or, 'What would happen if we added 8 (7, 6, etc.) successively and then found the sum of the digits?'. I suggested that they should investigate this problem and record their findings. At Measures the discoveries were well described by James (Table 9, page 97),|'When you add 9 repeatedly and then add the digits, ending with a single digit, you always get the same number. When you add 8, the sum of the digits decreases by 1. When you add 10, the sum of the digits increases by 1. When you add 7, the sum of the digits decreases by 2; when you add 11, the sum of the digits increases by 2. You always get all the digits in turn, but in different orders.'

Table 14: Digit sum when 9 is added repeatedly to a number fewer than 9 (6)

Number		Digit Sum
6		6
15		6
24		6
33		6
42		6
51		6
60		6
69	15→	6

Later on, I asked the children to record successive multiples of 3 and 9, and to find the sum of the digits. I hoped that the attention we gave to the repeating sum of the digits for multiples of 3 (3, 6, 9) would prevent them from including multiples of 3 amongst the prime numbers.

I told the children that there was a more complicated rule for recognizing multiples of 11, and asked them to look for this. I suggested that they should first concentrate on the multiples between 110 and 1000, and then look at four-digit numbers. Sheila at Meakins was the first in that group to say, 'The sum of the first and third digits is the middle digit'. For four-digit numbers Ruky said, 'If the sum of the first and third digits is the same as the sum of the second and fourth digits, the number is divisible by 11'.

(6) *Prime numbers*   I provided identical squares in one colour. I asked each pair to deal with a different range of numbers (up to 20), and to make all the possible rectangles (including squares) for each number in turn. For this activity both rectangles 1 × 2 and 2 × 1| ▢ ▢▢ were included for 2 (and so on for each subsequent number). The sequence began as shown in Figure 16, page 96. I then asked the children for their comments. The first comment was about the squares. 'The square numbers have an odd number of rectangles.' 'Always?', I enquired. '100 units would have rectangles: 100 by 1, 1 by 100; 50 by 2, 2 by 50; 25 by 4, 4 by 25; 20 by 5, 5 by 20; 10 by 10. That's nine rectangles. The set will always have one square so the number will be odd', was the usual reply. The subsequent comments usually referred to the two-rectangle numbers. I asked the children to describe these. Edward, at Movehall, said, 'Prime numbers are numbers which are not divisible by 2 or 3'. Later on, he extended his definition to include 5 and 7. Matthew at Makewell gave a more general description of primes: 'Each has factors of themselves and 1.' Some children made a useful table of primes and non-primes for reference (Table 15).

Table 15: Primes and non-primes

Number	No. of rectangles	Result
1	1	Not prime
2	2	prime
3	2	prime
4	3	Not prime
5	2	prime
6	4	Not prime
7	2	prime
8	4	Not prime
9	3	Not prime
10	4	Not prime
11	2	prime
12	6	Not prime

I then asked the children to make a six-day calendar for the months January, February and March, and to ring the prime numbers (Table 9, page 97).| At first, in all the groups, several multiples of 3 were ringed. Once more I asked them to write down successive multiples of 3 and to add the digits. Immediately they began to check the calendar numbers to see whether the digit sum was 3, 6 or 9. When the table was completed they described, without any difficulty, the position of the prime numbers after the first row, 'The primes come in columns 1 and 5. These columns also contain multiples of 5, or of 7, or of both'. James at Measures was fascinated by this discovery and made an eight-day calendar (Table 16) to see where the primes came. He also marked the primes in the ordinary seven-day calendar.

Table 16: Eight-day calendar by James

1	2	③	4	⑤	6	⑦	8
9	10	⑪	12	⑬	14	15	16
⑰	18	⑲	20	21	22	㉓	24
25	26	27	28	㉙	30	㉛	32
33	34	35	36	�37	38	39	40
㊶	42	㊸	44	45	46	㊼	48

(7) *Scale: cubes and squares*   Melia was the only school in which scale was studied during the first session. This was in response to a question. Peter asked, 'Am I right in saying, "If a farmer needed 4 kilograms of seed to sow one field, if he then sowed a field whose length and width were double those of the first field, the farmer would need 16 kilograms?"'. This problem gave me the opportunity to introduce three- and two-dimensional scale.

We began with three-dimensional models. I gave every child three interlocking cubes and asked them to make a model, and then to double all the dimensions. (As models we had a boot, a block of high-rise flats and a seat.) When, after a little difficulty, the models were correctly completed, I asked them to find the ratios of the volumes of the originals and their enlargements. They repeated this with the total skin (surface) areas of both. Immediately Nora asked, 'What does ratio mean? I've never heard of it.' (This happened with at least one child in every group.) I gave her my belt and asked her to mark on it my neck and waist perimeters. After explaining that ratio was the comparison of numbers or quantities by division, I asked the children what my $\frac{neck}{waist}$ ratio would be. Nora said, 'Your neck/waist ratio is ½. Your waist/neck ratio would be 2/1.' Daniel then said, 'The ratio of the volumes of the large and small models must be 8/1'. The ratio of the skin areas was harder to find. Eventually, they did this by comparing the areas of pairs of corresponding faces. They found that this ratio was 4/1.

They next made a scale model in which all the edges were trebled. They found that they had used 81 unit cubes. Steve said, 'The ratio of the volumes is 81 to 3: that's 27 to 1'.

I then asked the group to make a table showing their results for enlarging squares and cubes (Tables 17 and 18). I asked them to list and describe the units we used to measure volume and area. They found units of area particularly difficult to recall but eventually came up with square centimetres. The fourth years recognized the square numbers and the cube numbers but the third years did not. Robert pointed out that the square numbers differed by the 'odd number sequence'.

Pattern of the sequence of whole numbers

Numbers	0	1	2	3	4	5	6
Difference		1	1	1	1	1	1

Table 17: Pattern of the sequence of square numbers

Numbers	0	1	2	3	4	5	6
Square numbers	0	1	4	9	16	25	36
Difference		1	3	5	7	9	11
Second difference			2	2	2	2	2

Table 18: Patterns of the sequence of cube numbers

Numbers	0	1	2	3	4	5	6
Cube numbers	0	1	8	27	64	125	216
First difference		1	7	19	37	61	91
Second difference			6	12	18	24	30
Third difference				6	6	6	6

We then returned to the scale problems of the first session and discussed applications. I asked, 'When a baby elephant doubles its dimensions, is it enough if its foot dimensions are also doubled?' Peter said, 'When an elephant's dimensions are doubled, its weight is eight times what it was to start with. Its foot dimensions must be trebled to bear this weight. It can then carry nine times its original weight.' He illustrated his solution (Figure 22, page 104)| saying, 'An elephant's foot is almost square'.

As in the younger groups, I asked the children to make the largest square they could (without counting), using two handfuls of unit squares. They all built a square frame 'because a square frame will give the largest possible square'. They found four different methods of working out the number of unit squares used for square frames (Figure 13, page 80).| In the older groups the children quickly discovered the fifth method: subtracting the number of imagined square units in the inner square space from the number of units in the whole square (Figure 21, page 103). Patel at Meakins said, 'My large square has 7 by 7 units altogether. The inner square has 5 by 5 units. Take away 25 from 49 to get the number of units in the frame, that's 24.'

I tried, unsuccessfully, to get the children to express their methods in algebraic form. However Alec, at Missingham, was able to give a 'formula' for even numbers. He said, 'All even numbers have a factor 2. We could call even number $2s$; s could be any number.' 'How could you write any odd number then?', I asked. '$2s - 1$', said Alec. '$2s + 1$', said Donald. 'Can both be right?', I asked. Donald said, 'Yes, when $s = 0$, I get the first odd number, 1. Alec gets 1 when $s = 1$.'

I asked the children to find the patterns of the sequences of squares (Table 17) and of cubes (Table 18). At Missingham, some of the children had difficulty with the pattern of the cubes, until I reminded them that 'in mathematics you stop at nothing. You go on (adding, or finding differences or products or ratios) until you have to stop.' They were held up by the sequence 1, 7, 19, 37 .... When they continued with the next difference (6, 12, 18) they said, 'It's the table of 6s' (Table 18).

Donald, at Missingham, of his own accord used his calculating machine to enable him to find the difference patterns of the fourth and fifth powers of numbers. Before he started I asked him if he could predict what the constant numbers (the final difference) for the fourth and fifth powers would be. It took Donald only a few seconds to say, 'It will be 24 for fourth powers and 120 for fifth powers'. I was astonished at the speed with which Donald reached this solution. 'How did you arrive at this result?', I asked. 'Well', he answered, 'it's 2 for squares, that's 1×2; it's 6 for cubes, that's $1 \times 2 \times 3$. So it will be 24 for fourth powers, $1 \times 2 \times 3 \times 4$, and 120 for fifth powers, that's $1 \times 2 \times 3 \times 4 \times 5$.' Donald had a decided flair for pattern.

There were some children, particularly the third years, who found the next problem difficult to solve. With the group at Makewell I started on the abstract problem: 'Investigate the skin area/volume rate* of cubes of increasing sizes.' I described this problem as, 'finding how many squares were showing for each unit cube'. The children grew bored with this problem until we began to discuss the applications. I realized that I was wrong to assume that a group evidently interested in mathematics would be interested in an abstract problem in isolation from its context. For the rest of the groups I began with some applications.

For example, some of the children were discussing a news item: some babies had died in Buffalo (USA) because of the unusually low temperatures. I described what had happened in Britain in 1963 when we had six weeks of bitterly cold weather early in the year. Some babies had died because their mothers had put them outside in their prams. A notice appeared on the television screen: 'Mothers, do not put your babies out of doors in this cold weather. Their lungs cannot stand the cold.' Later on, an amended notice appeared. This read: 'Mothers, babies cannot survive outside in this cold weather because their skin area is so great compared with their size.' I told the children that the table they had made of squares and cubes would help them to understand this statement. When I suggested that they should look at what was happening to the skin area/volume rate as the cubes grew, one or two children in each group, for example, Fiesta at Measures, said at once that the product of the edge lengths (units) and the corresponding skin area/volume rate was always 6 (see Table 19).

Table 19: Skin area and volume of enlarging cubes

Edge length (cm)	1	2	3	4	5	6	x	
Base area (cm^2)	1	4	9	16	25	36	x^2	
Skin area (cm^2)	6	24	54	96	150	216	$6x^2$	
Volume (cm^3)	1	8	27	64	125	216	x^3	
$\dfrac{\text{Skin area}}{\text{Volume}}$ squares per cube	6	3	2	1.5	1.2	1	$\dfrac{6x^2}{x^3}$	$\to \dfrac{6}{x}$

---

* Ratio and rate are both comparisons by division. Ratio is a comparison by division of two (or more) numbers or like quantities in the same unit, e.g. lengths in metres, capacities in litres. Rate is a comparison by division of two different measures, e.g. price in pence per kilogram, speed in kilometres per hour, skin area per unit cube In a rate the units must be specified. A ratio is always a number.

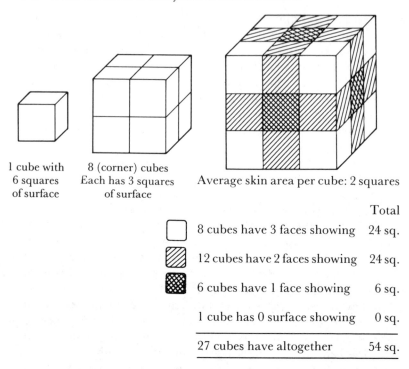

1 cube with
6 squares
of surface

8 (corner) cubes
Each has 3 squares
of surface

Average skin area per cube: 2 squares

		Total
☐	8 cubes have 3 faces showing	24 sq.
▨	12 cubes have 2 faces showing	24 sq.
▦	6 cubes have 1 face showing	6 sq.
	1 cube has 0 surface showing	0 sq.
	27 cubes have altogether	54 sq.

Figure 30: Surface area per unit cube for a sequence of cubes

This caused others to notice that when the edge length was doubled the rate was halved; when the edge length was trebled, the rate was divided by 3. However, some of the children were still puzzled about the concept: skin area/volume. I explained that it was easier to work with cubes as scale models than with human beings. I asked them to check that it was reasonable to consider a baby as the smallest (unit) cube and a man as the 3 by 3 by 3 cube. Alice, at Missingham, said that a baby could be 55 centimetres in length, then a man would be 165 centimetres tall (ratio 1 to 3). I then asked them each to make three cubes of edges 1, 2, 3 units with interlocking unit cubes. 'How many unit squares does the smallest cube have showing?' I asked (Figure 30). They all agreed that this was 6 unit squares. 'How many unit squares are showing altogether on the 2 by 2 by 2 cube?' was my next question. 'Four squares on each face, that's 24 squares altogether', was the answer. 'How many unit cubes are there?' I asked. 'Eight unit cubes', was the reply. 'So how many unit squares are showing for each unit cube?' was my next question. 'Three', was the answer. 'Does every unit cube in the 2 by 2 by 2 cube have 3 unit squares showing?', I asked. 'Yes', Alice answered, 'because each is a corner cube.' When we considered the 3 by 3 by 3 cube I suggested that the children should record the results each time. Alice suddenly intervened, 'There's a cube in the middle with no squares showing at all'. 'Are there any cubes with 3 unit squares showing?', I asked. Mary said, 'Yes, the 8 corner cubes all have 3 unit squares showing'. 'Are there any cubes with 2 unit squares showing?', I continued. This took longer. Steve noticed those at the middle of the top and bottom faces; Donald showed us the cubes at the corners of the middle layer, 12 cubes in all. Finally I asked whether there were any cubes with one unit square showing. Sheila said, 'There are 6 cubes, one at the middle of each face, with one square showing'. The children made a table of these results and checked that we had included all 27 of the cubes and all 54 of the faces. 'That's an average of two squares for every cube', Alec said. The group at Measures were excited by the results. Fiesta looked at the table of squares and cubes and said, 'A baby has 3 times as much skin showing for its size as a full grown man'. I asked, 'Why should the extent of skin area make it harder for babies to survive in extreme weather? What does the skin do?' Nora, at Melia, suggested, 'Our skin allows us to sweat when we are too hot. That keeps us cool.' She continued, after a pause, 'We lose energy when we get hot'. 'How do we replenish that energy?' I asked. Nora said, 'By eating'. I asked if that explained why small animals were unable to live all the year round in polar regions. 'Yes', Nora replied, 'there wouldn't be enough food for small creatures who need so much more food for their size'. James, at Measures, had brought an article to school about birds. It said that the wren needs its own weight in food each day to keep alive, whereas the blackbird needed one quarter of its weight. The children appreciated that the table of squares, cubes and the skin area/volume rate had many applications. We returned to this topic later on, when we made graphs of our results.

At Measures, this activity developed differently because James and Matthew immediately began to build hollow cubes. James insisted that this sequence began with a 2 by 2 by 2 cube 'because it has zero space inside'. They made a table showing the number of cubes they used for the 'shell' and the number of 'imaginary' cubes in the space.

Edge length of cube (cm)	2	3	4	5	6
No. of cubes used	8	20	32	44	56
No. of imaginary cubes in the space	0	7	32	81	160

They noticed the difference pattern of the numbers in the middle row. Then they looked for a pattern in the second and third sequences taken together. They first tried subtraction. 'There's no future in that', James said. When they added the pairs of numbers they recognized the pattern of the cubes at once. 'Of course', said Matthew, 'adding the rows must give the cubes because we are adding hollow shells and spaces inside.' They also tried to find different ways of building cubes; for example, starting with a cube at one corner, building round it and counting the number of cubes in each layer.

I then asked them how they could find their own volume. 'In the bath', was the usual answer. Nora, at Melia, said, 'I would measure it in centimetres'. We discovered that Nora was going to measure how much the water level rose. Daniel said, 'We must measure volume in litres – or in cubic decimetres'. At Meakins, Doreen suggested, 'Put 50 litres of water in the bath. Make a mark. Get in and make a second mark (for the new water level). Step out. Count the number of litres as you fill the bath from the lower to the higher mark.' All the groups described similar experiments for finding their own volumes. One boy persuaded his mother to help him carry out the experiment. His volume was 38 litres.

(8) *Containers and their cross-sections*   Because I planned to involve the children in an investigation into the areas and perimeters of sections of containers, I introduced the problem by using two plastic containers, one with an elliptical section and the other with a circular section. I began by asking the children whether the containers could be lifted without spilling when each was filled to the brim. The group at Meakins decided that the circular container could not be lifted without spilling, 'because it is heavy', said Sheila. I was surprised that these older children should have the same misconceptions as the younger ones. 'What do you mean by heavy?', I asked. 'About 500 grams', was the answer. 'Pick it up', I suggested. Sheila found that she had to use two hands, 'because I had to grasp it firmly', she said. Nevertheless, some water escaped.

'Now try the other one', I said. At first, Paul picked it up as shown in Figure 31. The water did not spill. He tried again; this time Jeremy watched the water level. 'The water has gone down', he commented.

Raoul suggested that Paul should pick the bottle up the other way round (see Figure 32). He did so and the water overflowed. At first, discussion centred on the type of plastic. The container with a circular section was a yoghurt pot made of pliable plastic; the other container was a distilled water bottle made of tough, more rigid plastic. Paul said, 'The plastic used for the water bottle is tougher than that used for the yoghurt pot'. 'Why?' I asked. 'You have to use the water bottle more often', said Ruky. I wanted the children to find out why the water level went down when Paul picked the bottle up in the first way, so I directed their attention to the different shapes of the sections by asking, 'What is the same about the rim of the yoghurt pot (its largest section) and the largest section of the bottle?' (There was a ball of fine string on the table.) At first all the groups were baffled by this question, but eventually each group thought of comparing the perimeters of the two sections. These were almost identical; 28 centimetres.

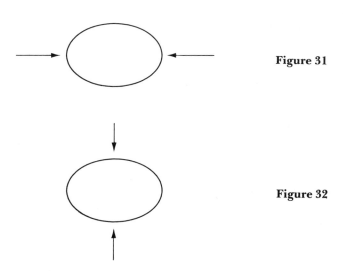

Figure 31

Figure 32

I then asked the groups which section would have the larger area, the ellipse or the circle. All agreed that the circle would be larger. 'How shall we check?', I asked. The yoghurt pot was easy: they turned it upside down on squared paper, drew round the rim and counted the squares. But Donald, at Missingham, had another idea. He first calculated the radius of a circle of circumference 28 centimetres. Then he used my calculating machine to find the area of the circle from the formula (which he checked with me) $\pi \times$ radius squared. The others checked their answer, found by counting squares (66 sq cm) with Donald's (62 sq cm).

Tracing the section of the water bottle was more difficult. The widest section was part-way up. The children at Melia used a long pencil to trace the section (Figure 33). Steve began to think that the ellipse might be larger in area. He found its area to be 56 sq cm. Robert made a square with the same perimeter and found that its area was 49 sq cm. Nora thought a triangle could have a larger area. At this stage I asked all the groups (except Movehall) to find the shape of the rectangle with the largest area. The children started with the perimeter of 28 centimetres and gave me, at random, the dimensions of possible rectangles. Then I asked them to make a table with the rectangles in order. (I had suggested that they should use whole numbers for the edges.) By that time all the children realized that the square had the largest area of all rectangles with the same perimeter. We then returned to the problem about the two containers with the same perimeter. Why had the water level in the elliptical container

Figure 33

gone down when the container was lifted as in Figure 31? The children at Meakins concluded, 'The elliptical section has a smaller area than the circular section with the same perimeter. The water is sucked in because when you press the narrowest sides the section is nearer circular so the bottle can hold more water. If you press the longer sides you make it more elongated and less like a circle, so the water comes out.'

But Nora, at Melia, still thought that she might be able to make a triangle, with perimeter 28 centimetres, the area of which was greater than that of the circle. So I gave the children in this and the other groups loops of string of perimeter 28 centimetres and asked them to investigate the areas of triangles with this perimeter.

At Missingham the children soon realised that the question was too open. 'We must fix something', said Donald. Edwin put two fingers on the string to hold it in position, thus making a base. As Alec moved a pencil round, holding the string taut, Edwin said, 'The pencil is drawing a circle'. 'Are you sure?', I asked. Alec experimented by using two drawing pins to fix the base. He moved these farther apart and pulled the string taut with the pencil, drawing a curve (Figure 34). Edwin saw that the shape made was not a circle. He said, 'The pencil has traced an oval this time'. Alec continued to experiment, moving the drawing pins nearer together and farther apart. Finally he said, 'You get a circle when one drawing pin is on top of the other'. 'What happens when the pins are farthest apart?' I asked. 'You get a line, no area at all', was the reply.

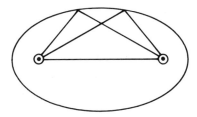

Figure 34

We returned to the triangles. Santos at Movehall said, 'The equilateral triangle must have the largest area of all for this perimeter', but he could not give a reason. 'When the base is fixed', I asked, 'which triangle has the greatest area?' Santos suggested, 'The triangle at the top, because it comes midway between the zero area positions'. I asked them how they could find the area of a triangle. Donald, at Missingham, who made a collection of formulae, said, 'It's half base times height'. When I asked how he had arrived at this formula Donald said, 'You draw the enclosing rectangle'. The others in the group checked this (Figure 35). Alec showed how the method

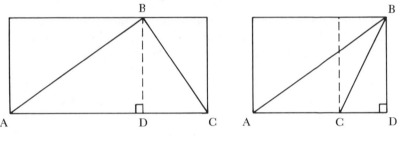

Figure 35   **Figure 36**

could be made to work for obtuse angled triangles (Figure 36). Sally, with some hesitation, said that the triangle with the greatest height must have the greatest area 'because all the triangles have the same base'. They found that this triangle always had two edges equal – it was isosceles (Donald). I asked Sally to find the triangle with the greatest area on base BC (triangle ABC). Then Alice took over. 'Now we'll use base AC' (triangle ASC). By now the children were excited. Mary changed the base again (SC). 'The triangle is nearly equilateral', they exclaimed. After one more change of base the triangle was indistinguishable from an equilateral triangle (Figure 37, triangle TSC). So no more changes of base could be made. The triangle now had maximum area with this perimeter.

At Melia, the children continued the investigation into areas of triangles with the same perimeter still farther. They decided to find the shape of the largest isosceles triangle by another method. Daniel

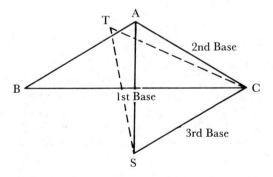

Figure 37

found two positions where isosceles triangles had zero area (Figure 38, XY and PQ). He suggested that halfway between these two positions (XY and PQ) the isosceles triangle would have the greatest area. He found that in this position the triangle was not equilateral, so he knew that his suggestion was not correct. Santos, at Movehall, also guessed halfway. The problem was too difficult for them to solve by this method.

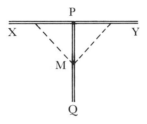

Figure 38

The groups at Missingham and Measures investigated the perimeters of rectangles with the same areas, and of other shapes. I gave every child six identical sheets of paper and asked them to put a single fold in each to divide the paper into halves. Each fold had to be different from the others. I explained that at least one fold would have to be an estimate. At Measures, while James was making a second fold in the paper to test his estimate, he exclaimed, 'The two folds cross at the centre of the paper'. 'Does this always happen?', I asked. The children made second folds in the other sheets; every pair of folds crossed at the centre. 'How many folds do you think you could make?', was my next question. 'As many as you like, but the folds must all go through the centre of the sheet', James said. I then asked the children to cut along one of the oblique folds (not the diagonal) and to see what they had to do to check that one half was identical with the other. James and Matthew, unlike the others, immediately rotated one piece about the centre of the paper through half a turn (Figure 39). I was surprised that these two boys saw the solution so quickly. I asked if they had heard about rotational symmetry before. 'We've done quite a lot of it', they said. The others turned one half over, found that it did not fit the other half that way, so turned it over again, and rotated it until the two halves coincided. They soon realized that turning the paper over twice meant that they need not turn it over at all! They then rotated one piece through half a turn as the two boys had done.

Next I asked them how many different shapes they could make by matching edges from the cut pieces, and how many of these had either mirror or rotational symmetry. 'Four shapes have mirror symmetry [Figure 41] and four have rotational' [Figure 40] , Hazel answered. 'Are the perimeters the same?' I asked. 'No, but the areas are', the group at Measures replied unanimously. They soon decided which were the two shapes with the longest perimeter (Figures 40, 41, d and D) and which were the shapes with the shortest perimeter (Figures 40, 41, a,c and A,c). They repeated the experiment with the diagonal fold (Figures 42 and 43).

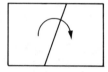

Figure 39: Oblique fold

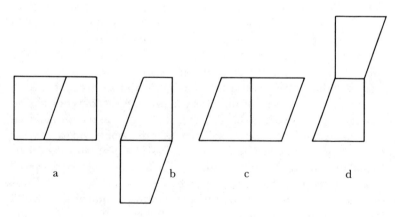

Figure 40: Four shapes with rotational symmetry

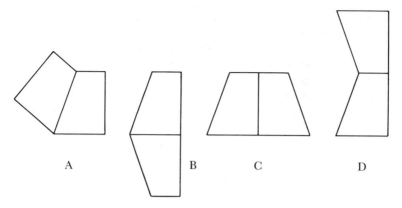

Figure 41: Four Shapes with mirror symmetry
> One piece of paper is turned over to obtain these shapes. d and D
> have the longest perimeters. a and A have the shortest perimeters.

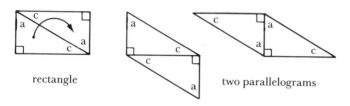

rectangle   two parallelograms

Figure 42: Three shapes with rotational symmetry: Diagonal fold

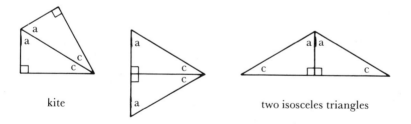

kite   two isosceles triangles

Figure 43: Three shapes with mirror symmetry

At Missingham, Edwin said, 'The perimeters will be the same because the areas are the same'. 'Are you sure?', I asked. Edwin hesitated. 'Find two different shapes with the longest perimeters', I suggested. Edwin said, 'I'll have to put the shortest sides together to find the shape with the longest perimeter'. 'How do you know which sides are shortest?', I asked. Alec replied, 'It's the perpendicular height. All slant lines are longer.' He pointed out the longest lines. I had suggested that before working with the two identical triangles, the children should colour edges of the same length in one colour, and similarly equal angles in one colour. When I asked the children to make, and describe, shapes with matching edges, Alice was the first to make and recognize a parallelogram (Figure 42). She said, 'Its opposite sides are equal'. I asked her to justify this. 'Measure the sides', she said. I explained that I could not accept measuring as a mathematical justification. Then Alice remembered that she had cut two identical triangles, and had marked in the equal edges. 'The opposite angles are equal, too', she said. 'Show me another shape with the same perimeter', I said.

Donald made a 'triangle'. 'It's isosceles', he added (Figure 43). 'How can you satisfy me that it is a triangle?', I asked. 'The base might not be a straight line'. 'But it is', said Mary. 'The two angles in the base are right angles, because they are angles at the corners of a rectangle'. They discovered that the rectangle and the kite both had the shortest perimeter.

The groups at both Missingham and Measures told their teachers that they had enjoyed this activity.

(9) *Graphical representation and limits**   Throughout the sessions we represented discoveries by diagrams and block or line graphs whenever practicable. All the third years were familiar with block graphs but none of them had made line graphs.

(a) *Straight line graphs.* We began by representing the multiplication tables, using the same scale on both axes. The third years used identical interlocking cubes, the fourth years made line graphs. I asked the third years to describe their block graphs. 'They make equal steps', they said. The fourth years said that they had plotted number pairs; for the table of twos they plotted (1,2), (2,4) and so on. I asked, 'Are you justified in joining the points? Can you name any number pairs which belong to this relationship but are not whole numbers?' I was immediately given ($\frac{1}{2}$,1), ($\frac{1}{4}$,$\frac{1}{2}$), ($\frac{1}{10}$, $\frac{1}{5}$), and many more. 'Do all the

---

* To facilitate reduction in the size of graphs in this book centimetre/millimetre paper has been frequently used. For many of the graphs centimetre squared paper is more suitable for children to use – and is usually cheaper.

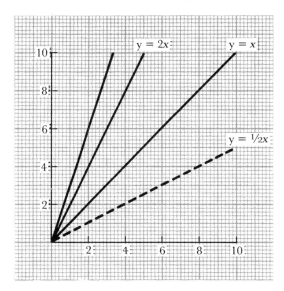

Figure 44

on your line graphs belong to that line?' (Figure 44). Donald at Missingham checked this and volunteered that the equations of the multiplication tables were: '$y = x$, $y = 2x$, $y = 3x$, and so on'. 'Tell me about $y = x$', I asked. Donald said, '$y = x$ is the one times table' (Figure 44). The third years then drew the line graphs of the multiplication tables. I asked if anyone could suggest a multiplication table to occupy the empty section of the graph. It was some time before Nora at Melia suggested the table of ½s. Peter, at the same school, described the 'multiplication table' graphs as 'the diagonals of oblongs'. He said, 'The one times table is the diagonal of a square'.

When the groups drew graphs of the relationships in their table of squares and cubes, some children in all the groups predicted that the perimeter graph would be a straight line 'because it's the four times table, they are all multiples of four. The steps are equal'.

(b) *Graphs which are curves.* The children at first predicted that the line graph of the square numbers would be straight 'because the differences are all 2'. (The children were, of course, referring to the differences of the differences, not to the odd number series which constitutes the first difference.) I suggested that they should make a block graph of the square numbers. Some of the children were surprised to see that the steps were not equal (Figure 45). Then they remembered that the steps were the odd number sequence and that their differences were 2. Alice at Melia reminded the group that she had discovered, 'The difference between successive numbers in the number sequence is 1, in one step. The difference between square numbers is 2, in two steps. The difference between cube numbers is 6, in three steps, and so on' (Tables 17, 18, page 125).

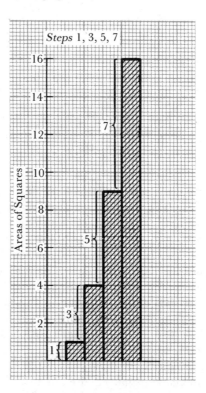

Figure 45: Block graph of the area of squares

When the children at Makewell had made line graphs of the squares and cubes, using the same axes, (Figure 46), they were surprised to find that both curves passed through the points (1,1) and (0,0). They asked, 'What happens to the curves between these two points? They seem very close together'. I suggested that Hazel and Nora should make an enlargement of the section of the graph from 0 to 1. I gave them millimetre squared paper and they decided to plot the squares and cubes for the points (0.1,0.01), (0.2,0.04) as far as 0.9 for the squares, and (0.1,0.001), (0.2,0.008) ... for the cubes. (This gave them good practice in multiplying decimals and in confirming once more that when a number is multiplied by a decimal fraction it decreases in size.) They finally used the scale: 10 mm for 0.1 on both axes (Figure

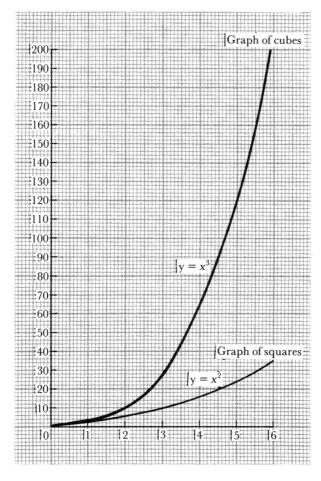

Figure 46: Squares and cubes between 0 and 6

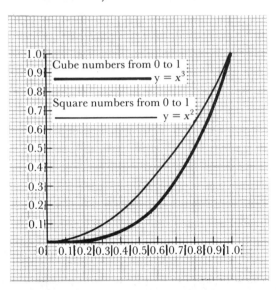

Figure 47: Squares and cubes between 0 and 1

47). When they discussed with the others in the group what they had done, they concluded, 'Squares of numbers between 0 and 1 are always greater than the cubes. After 1, the cubes are greater than the squares.' 'How does your graph show this?' I asked. Nora said, 'The squares are all above the cubes on this graph. On our first graph the cubes were above the squares.'

Donald, at Missingham, first made a graph of $y = x^3$ with mirror symmetry (top section of Figure 48). I asked him what $(-1)^3$ or $(-1) \times (-1) \times (-1)$ would be. 'Oh', he said, 'It's negative 1, so the graph will have rotational symmetry!' (The black line in Figure 48 shows the graph of $y = x^3$.)

All the groups also drew the graph of number pairs in Table 20.

Table 20

edge length cm	1	2	3	4	5	6
skin area/volume	6	3	2	1½	1.2	1

They had already noticed that the products of corresponding number pairs were 6 and also that the relation was inverse: when

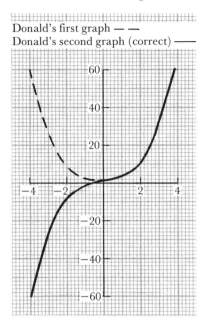

Donald's first graph — —
Donald's second graph (correct) ——

Figure 48: y = x³

the edge length was doubled, the skin area/volume rate was halved, etc. No one was able to predict what the graph would look like. They were surprised by its shape (Figure 49). Donald, at Missingham, said that its axis of symmetry was *y* = *x*. I discussed with each group the values of the skin area/volume rate when the edge length was ½ (12), $\frac{1}{10}$ (60), $\frac{1}{100}$ (600). Neal, at Makewell, said, 'The graph will continue getting nearer to the axis but it will never touch it'. This showed that Neal had a clear insight into the concept of a mathematical limit. They also calculated what was happening to the skin area/volume rate when the edge was very large.

(c) *Varied ways of representing an investigation.* The activity which was represented in the widest variety of ways was the investigation into the areas of shapes with the same perimeter.

(i) At Melia, where the children had first superimposed a circle and an ellipse of perimeter 28 centimetres to compare the areas, they displayed the shapes, traced on squared paper, in order of area. Daniel had found the area of the circle (62 sq cm),

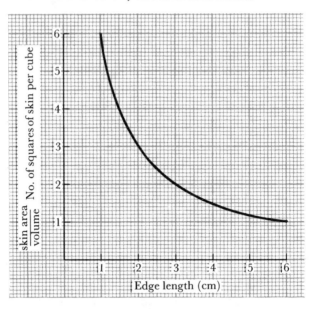

Figure 49: Graph of $\frac{\text{skin area}}{\text{volume}}$ rate for enlarging cubes

Steve the area of the ellipse (55 sq cm), Robert the area of the square (49 sq cm) and Nora the area of a triangle (36 sq cm).

(ii) The children in all the groups made a table showing all the rectangles with perimeters 20 cm having a whole number of centimetres for their edges (Table 11, page 107). They found the difference pattern of the areas: 9, 7, 5, 3, 1. The children at Melia noticed at once that this pattern was like the difference pattern of successive squares. 'It's the odd number pattern again', Daniel said. 'Tell me the difference pattern of the square numbers', I said. 'It's 1, 3, 5, 7, 9', was the response. 'You've told me how the two patterns are alike. How are they different?', I asked. 'They're going the other way', said Steve. I asked Steve to make his statement more mathematical. He said, 'In the square numbers the odd number differences increase; in the areas of the rectangles the odd number differences decrease'. 'Does the odd number difference for the rectangles decrease all the time?' I asked. Steve said, 'We said that the pattern went on: 1, 3, 5, but it was really -1, -3, -5. The numbers were all decreasing by two each time.'

Table 21: Width, length and areas of rectangles with perimeter 20 cm, showing difference pattern of|areas

Width cm	length cm	area sq cm	differences
0	10	0	
			9
1	9	9	
			7
2	8	16	
			5
3	7	21	
			3
4	6	24	
			1
5	5	25	
			−1
6	4	24	
			−3
7	3	21	
			−5
8	2	16	
			−7
9	1	9	
			−9
10	0	0	

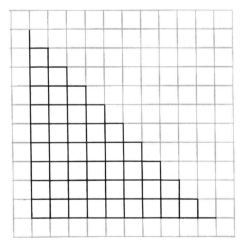

Figure 50: Overlapping rectangles with perimeter 20cm.
Compare with Figure 24

Each pair of children cut out (from centimetre squared paper) a complete set of the rectangles in Table 21. I asked them to arrange the rectangles in order. In every group one pair of children arranged the rectangles symmetrically (Figure 24, page 108). They described this representation: 'The rectangles all have the same perimeter. Their widths first increase, then decrease. The square has the largest area' (Ruky and Sheila at Meakins). Patel and Jeremy arranged their rectangles in order of increasing widths (Figure 25, page 108). I asked them what was happening to the heights. Jeremy said, 'The heights are decreasing all the time'. I asked Doreen to keep the rectangles in the same arrangement as Jeremy and Patel but to overlap them, pushing them to the lower left hand corner of the paper (Figure 50). When I asked Doreen to describe her arrangement she said, 'The top right hand corners of the rectangles go down in equal steps. They are in a straight line.' I asked her to make an addition square for pairs of numbers from 1 to 10 (Table 22 below). She shaded the squares containing 10 and said, 'The 10s in the addition table are like my pattern of rectangles'. (In Table 22 the line of 10s shows number pairs with a sum of 10. Figure 51 shows rectangles the sum of whose width and length – half perimeter – is also 10 units.)

Table 22: Addition of number pairs from the set 1 to 10

10	11	12	13	14	15	16	17	18	19	20
9	10	11	12	13	14	15	16	17	18	19
8	9	10	11	12	13	14	15	16	17	18
7	8	9	10	11	12	13	14	15	16	17
6	7	8	9	10	11	12	13	14	15	16
5	6	7	8	9	10	11	12	13	14	15
4	5	6	7	8	9	10	11	12	13	14
3	4	5	6	7	8	9	10	11	12	13
2	3	4	5	6	7	8	9	10	11	12
1	2	3	4	5	6	7	8	9	10	11
+	1	2	3	4	5	6	7	8	9	10

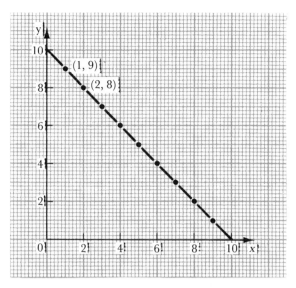

Figure 51: Graph of x + y = 10

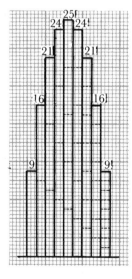

**Figure 52: Area of rectangles of perimeters 20cm
represented by a block graph (sq cm)**

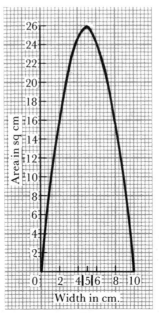

Donald recorded: This graph is y = x (10 − x)
where y is area, x is width

**Figure 53: Graph of areas of rectangles
with perimeter of 20cm**

At Missingham, Donald plotted the numbers (0,10), (1,9), (2,8), etc. He joined the points (Figure 51) saying, 'All the half values like (½,9½) will be in this line. Its equation is x + y = 10.' He also drew a line graph for the (width, area) values from Table 21. He described his graph (Figure 53), 'As the widths of the rectangles increase, the area increases to a maximum, when it is a square. Then the area decreases to zero. It started at zero, too.'

I asked Sheila and Doreen at Meakins to make a block graph of the areas of the rectangles. They looked puzzled. 'What is a characteristic of block graphs?', I asked. Sheila said, 'The blocks are the same width'. But it was Doreen who thought of placing the strips for each rectangle end to end (Figure 52). I asked them what their block graph and the line graph had in common. Sheila said, 'They both show that the greatest area is 25 square centimetres'.

Table 23: Perimeters of rectangles with area 16 sq cm

width cm	length cm	perimeter cm
1	16	34
2	8	20
4	4	16
8	2	20
16	1	34

Table 24: Products of pairs of numbers 1 to 12

	Products of 36				Products of 16			Products of 12			
12	[12]	24	(36)	48	60	72	84	96	108	120	132	144
11	11	22	33	44	55	66	77	88	99	110	121	132
10	10	20	30	40	50	60	70	80	90	100	110	120
9	9	18	27	(36)	45	54	63	72	81	90	99	108
8	8	(16)	24	32	40	48	56	64	72	80	88	96
7	7	14	21	28	35	42	49	56	63	70	77	84
6	6	[12]	18	24	30	(36)	42	48	54	60	66	72
5	5	10	15	20	25	30	35	40	45	50	55	60
4	4	8	[12]	(16)	20	24	28	32	(36)	40	44	48
3	3	6	9	[12]	15	18	21	24	27	30	33	(36)
2	2	4	6	8	10	[12]	14	(16)	18	20	22	24
1	1	2	3	4	5	6	7	8	9	10	11	[12]
×	1	2	3	4	5	6	7	8	9	10	11	12

The groups at Movehall and Measures made a similar range of representations to show how the perimeters varied for a set of rectangles of area 36 sq cm. (In all the diagrams, for the sake of simplicity, we have shown rectangles of 16 sq cm; the children worked with areas of 16 and 36 sq cm.) The representations included:

(1) Table 23 showing the width, length and perimeters of rectangles of area 16 sq cm.

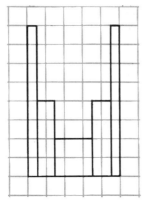

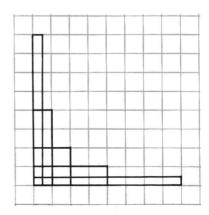

Figure 54:
Symmetrical arrangement
of cut rectangles

Figure 56: Rectangles overlapping

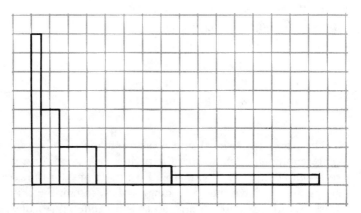

Figure 55: Rectangles arranged in order of increasing width,
decreasing length

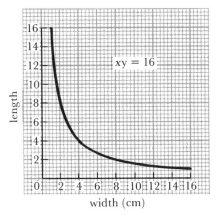

Figure 57: Line graph length/width of rectangles

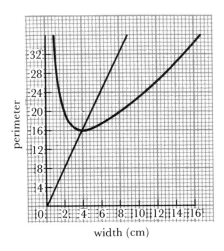

width (cm)

Figure 58: Graph of perimeters (See Table 23)

(2) A symmetrical arrangement of the set of these rectangles (Figure 54).

(3) The rectangles arranged in increasing order of width (Figure 55). The children noticed at once that this was an inverse relation: when the width was doubled, the height was halved, etc.

(4) The rectangles overlapping (Figure 56).

(5) Table 24 showing products of pairs of numbers 1 to 12. Products 16, 12 and 36 were shaded in.

(6) Line graph of the (width, length) from Table 23, $xy = 16$ (Figure 57).

(7) Jo, at Measures, cut string perimeters, using Table 23.

(8) One pair in each group plotted the number pairs (width, perimeter), Figure 58. The graph surprised them. Santos, at Movehall, said, 'The table (23) made us expect the graph to look symmetrical but it doesn't'. Finally, after much discussion, they offered an explanation, 'In the table we used whole numbers only, so some points are missing'. Phiroz at Measures described his graph, 'The perimeter decreases to a minimum when the shape is a square. Then it increases.' I asked both groups whether they could find an axis of symmetry for the perimeter graph. Maria at Movehall and Phiroz at Measures both found an axis of mirror symmetry by cutting along the curve and folding.

(10) *Miscellaneous problems*   During the final session I gave the groups two further problems:

(a) Investigate what happens when you either place a coloured peg between hinged mirrors, or draw a line between the mirrors, and try to make regular shapes.

(b) Investigate triangular numbers.

(a) At Movehall, after I had allowed time for experimenting with the hinged mirrors, I began by asking, 'Could you use the hinged mirrors, and the line, to make a square when you look into the mirrors?' Santos said he could, but he had to make several attempts. He said, 'The mirrors have to be at right angles' (Figure 59). Carl said he would make an equilateral triangle. Again, it was some time before Carl was satisfied. He measured the angle between the mirrors; it was 120 degrees. Daphne made an octagon; the angle between the mirrors was 45 degrees this time. Santos entered the results in a table. He said,

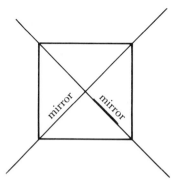

Figure 59

'When the number of edges is doubled the angle is halved. So it's an inverse relation.' By now the children knew what type of graph to expect.

At Makewell, I had decided to provide hinged mirrors with a red peg between them. Unfortunately, I had forgotten to bring protractors. After the children had experimented with the material I explained what I had forgotten. Mark suggested, 'Why don't we fold a piece of paper? We could make 90 degrees, 45 degrees and 135 degrees just by folding.' But when I gave the children paper for folding they could not think how to fold a sheet of paper to halve the angle at the corner. Nora was the first to think of matching the edges of the paper to bisect the right angle. Adrian made a table for the angles we could make between the mirrors (Table 25). He said, 'When the number of images is halved the angle between the mirrors is doubled'. (We always included the object when we were counting the images.) All the children made a graph of the number pairs shown in Table 25. (Before they had completed these I had managed to borrow some protractors, so we were able to check the angles.) They recognized the shape of the graph and wanted to join the points. 'You've drawn a graph showing the angle between the mirrors when you can see 2, 3, 4, 5, etc. pegs. Could you give a meaning to every point on a line graph? What would 2½ pegs mean?', I asked. Adrian said, 'Could we put in a dotted line? We just want to see what the graph looks like.' When this was done, I asked what operation they could use on the number pairs in the table which would give the same answer for all the pairs. They soon found that the operation was multiplication.

Table 25

No. of edges	Angle between mirrors
3	120°
4	90°
5	72°
6	60°
8	45°

Figure 60: Triangular numbers
What is the next one?
Is there a triangular number
before three?
Is 100 a trangular number?
(Chemists use a triangle for
counting out pills.)

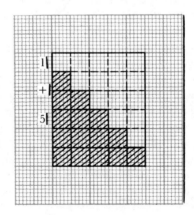

Figure 61

(b) At Melia Nora was using identical counters to make triangular numbers. I asked her if she could think of a way of finding the sum of the numbers 1 to 5. Both Nora and Daniel had made successive rows of unit squares to represent the numbers 1 to 5. 'What would happen if you combine your two sets of rows?', I asked. Daniel arranged the two sets 'top to tail', as in Figure 61. Nora said, 'The sum is $\frac{1}{2}$ $(1 + 5) \times 5$'. I asked them to find the sum of the numbers 1 to 10. Nora said, 'That will be $\frac{1}{2}$ $(1 + 10) \times 10$. That's 55.'

(11) *Reinforcement*   As I had expected, for the able children as well as for the slow learners, one discovery (for example, of a number pattern) was not enough to make the learning permanent. When the able children found the patterns of square and of cube numbers, and of their differences, they soon forgot the sequences and the patterns, unless I provided a sufficient variety of activities in which the patterns could be applied. (Perhaps this was not surprising in view of the intervals between the sessions – one or two weeks.)

I set the children several problems in which the sequences could be used. I also gave them a variety of activities in order to assess whether they understood what they were doing and could apply the sequences.

As with the younger groups I gave the older children ordering and sorting activities which involved a set of cards, 0 to 16. (See Figures 17 and 18, pages 99 and 100). These children had no difficulty in accepting that zero is a multiple of two. However, they were more reluctant to accept zero as a square number, although ultimately they were persuaded by the pattern of square numbers. We returned to this concept when the children made line graphs of square and cube numbers. Some of them were more ready to include zero in the set of square numbers when they drew the graph of the squares of positive and negative numbers 'because you can't have a gap in the middle of the graph', they argued.

III. Findings from the sessions

The children in the able groups, particularly the older children, were most responsive – and often uninhibited – in the suggestions they made for the solutions of problems. Some of them showed a mathematical insight which I had not expected. For example, Donald, at Missingham, who predicted that the largest triangle would be the isosceles triangle midway between the positions of zero area; Neal at Makewell, who realized that the graph of an inverse relationship would never meet the axis, however small the x-value was.

Even the children who had said that they preferred working on their own, or working from a textbook 'because books always told you exactly what to do', could not resist joining in when the problems interested them. Moreover, they became accustomed to using material and making the best use of it (although some of them had decried it initially). Most of these children had the confidence to meet a challenge. The questions had to be sufficiently open to allow for a variety of responses, yet they had to make demands commensurate with the children's intelligence. To say to these children, 'Are you sure?' was a stimulus rather than a discouragement. (The intonation of this question makes a great deal of difference. It should imply doubt but not criticism.)

I soon noticed a change in the children's use of mathematical vocabulary. They began to use mathematical terminology rather than less well defined expressions to describe sequences; for example, 'The numbers increased by 2 each time, starting with 1 and finishing with 11', etc. They became far more flexible, too, in the solutions they suggested. As they gained confidence, they became self-critical and were happy to have their solutions appraised by the group.

IV. Discussion

All the activities and investigations I used were new to the older children, as were the methods of oral questioning and discussion. They were unaccustomed to the emphasis on problem-solving, and to the sustained investigations which formed the major part of the last few sessions.

With the exception of the groups at Melia, Meakins and Makewell, the attitudes of the third and fourth years towards the mathematics sessions became unpredictable during the second half of the summer term. The fourth years grew more unsettled and sometimes aggressive as they became increasingly apprehensive about their new schools. In consequence, the confidence of the third years seemed to diminish still further.

In two schools, during the summer term of 1977, I had third years only for one session while the fourth years were on a school journey. They took the opportunity first to say how much they had enjoyed the session on their own, and then to reveal their attitudes to working with fourth years. At Measures, there were four able, confident and responsive boys (one a third year). The three girls (two from the third year) were often shy and reticent. (They would never respond when the tape recorder was switched on.) During the seventh session Jane had said, 'I don't like maths anyway'. Lucy said, 'We prefer [the work card system recently adopted in the third year]. It uses more apparatus.' When I pressed Lucy to give me an example of an activity she had enjoyed, she said, 'Measure the building'. (It was the first time in the new scheme that they had been given practical work of this kind.) I realized that the investigation I had given on scale (using sequences of cubes) was difficult for the third years, particularly since the boys had shown so much enthusiasm. When, during the eighth session, the third years were on their own, Lucy said, 'We enjoyed it today. Sometimes we're put off by the boys. They dominate the sessions and make suggestions we do not understand. We're not as good as the boys.' Nothing I could say would persuade the girls that their potential was as good as that of the boys! At the final session all the group said that they had enjoyed everything. Jane said, 'I like coming and did not dislike what we did'.

In contrast, at Meakins (where there were five girls and three boys in the group), Doreen said, 'I don't enjoy [the card system] but I do enjoy what we do in these sessions'. Sheila continued, 'When we discuss and exchange methods we think of even more ways of doing things'. But this group, too, lost some of their impetus towards the end of the summer term. The intense concentration required for the sustained investigation seemed too much, even for the ablest girl.

At Makewell, the final verdict was, 'We enjoyed everything. It was a change from the maths we usually have.' At Melia, the enjoyment was unqualified. Nora, the only girl, a fourth year, was completely at ease in the group; all the boys respected her ability.

I had special problems with the older groups at two schools. At Missingham three very able boys were misfits in the group. Donald, who 'had a passion' for mathematics, worked at home from an advanced textbook. He frequently used mathematical formulae which the others did not understand. But they were used to him and I was usually able to persuade him to make his contribution in simpler mathematical language. Alec pronounced, at the first session, that he disliked working with others and much preferred to be on his own. At the same session, Steve objected to using materials. Nevertheless, these boys made outstanding contributions and worked well throughout the sessions. One boy said at the final session that he had enjoyed nothing. By contrast, Alice, a fourth year girl, said, 'I enjoyed everything'. Doreen, a third year girl, explained when the third years were on their own, 'It's difficult for third years to work with fourth years, especially since the fourth years are all boys'.

At Movehall, an able fourth year girl was responsible for the disaffection which sometimes erupted in the group. She made no bones about her resentment at having to work with children who were not as quick at mathematics as she was. (Unfortunately, her sister, a third year, was also in this group.) An able fourth year boy had said, 'Using cubes is babyish'. However, he made good use of the material I provided whenever he saw that it would help him to arrive at a solution.

A third year boy was most affected by the atmosphere which pervaded the group at times. He asked, 'Why do I have to come? I'm no good at maths and I dislike it. I can't think why I was chosen.'

I discussed the problems within this group with the head. He joined us one day to give the group a chance to air their grievances. The third year girls said, 'We don't mind coming but it's boring sometimes'. The third year boy said, 'I enjoy very little in maths'. Santos said, 'I've no strong feelings but I prefer written problems'.

At the final session Maria, as usual, came unwillingly and showed her bad temper. I sent her away – for the first time. Immediately the mood of the group changed; we had an exhilarating and successful session, as all the children reported to their teachers. I had continued working with Maria because of my research project but the group's responses during the final session made me realize that this had been unfair to the other members of the group.

The unpredictable attitudes of the older groups seemed not to affect their achievement to any great extent. The majority of the 48 children who attended the sessions were imaginative and very responsive. They convinced me that they were able to tackle problems and investigations far in advance of any work they were being given by their teachers at that time.

V. Interviews with the children after their transfer to the high schools

At the end of the summer term, 1977, I sent the names of the able children with whom I had worked during the two preceding terms to the heads of the mathematics departments at the two high schools. I indicated which pupils had made outstanding contributions to the mathematical investigations I provided. Only two of the pupils outstanding at mathematics in my groups had transferred to the two project high schools.

I arranged termly interviews with these children to try to determine to what extent the special needs of the able pupils were being met. I hoped that I would gain some insight into what the pupils were learning in mathematics, whether they were enjoying it, the balance between new topics and consolidation, and the teaching methods used. Since the teachers of the first year pupils at the high schools had attended the first input of the working sessions for middle school teachers during my research project, these interviews with the pupils might help me to assess whether the first input had had any effect on their teaching of mathematics at that stage. As a result of these interviews I would be able to discuss with the heads and the heads of the mathematics departments the extent to which the pupils appeared to have settled to the new routine in general, and their reactions to the mathematics they were doing.

I made some disturbing discoveries. The problem the schools had failed to solve was the treatment of the pupils who were outstanding at mathematics. I had suggested to the heads of departments that these two required mathematics appropriate to their exceptional potential if they were to retain their intense interest in the subject. The heads of departments agreed, and possible mathematics books for the pupils to use, mainly for study on their own, were discussed. I also pressed both heads of department to ascertain for themselves the potential of each boy and to take some personal responsibility for his mathematical education, perhaps giving him one session on his own every week or fortnight.

This suggestion was necessary at both schools but for different reasons. At one high school the two pupils most outstanding at mathematics were being taught by a new teacher without qualifications in the subject. When I discussed the pupils with her she told me that she was anxious that they should not outstrip her own knowledge. I understood her difficulty at this early stage of her career. In response to the question, 'Have you ever had any difficulty with mathematics?', one of the boys said at my first interview with him, 'Yes – negative numbers. The teacher's explanation was not clear. It took me quite a few minutes to understand. I didn't like to ask. I prefer to work things out for myself .... The pace is slow – but it was even slower at the middle school.'

Eventually, after much pressure on my part, the head of the mathematics department at this school interviewed all the able pupils in the following June – nine months after they had first entered the school. He immediately started two of them on advanced mathematics (A-level). These pupils could easily have lost their interest in the subject entirely during the nine-month interval.

At the second high school the able mathematics set was taught by a graduate mathematics teacher of long experience. At successive interviews the other outstanding pupil from my able group commented as follows. After the first month: 'Maths is disappointing. The teacher is very strict and makes us use her methods.' Two months later on he said, 'I've got over that problem; I present my work so beautifully that no teacher could criticize my method. I'm happier now because most days I go to Maths Club and work on the computer. [The Mathematics Department generously organized and staffed a Maths Club for four lunch hours each week.] And I enjoy science, we have more freedom there.' During the following term, 'She's [the mathematics teacher] alright when you get to know her. The methods she teaches us are good. I don't go to the Maths Club now. There's not enough to do.' (He had made and used several computer programmes.)

In the third term he said, 'I've been glad of the chance to consolidate what I did last year at the middle school ... Sometimes the teacher here gives me different work and [the teacher responsible for mathematics in the first year] gives me problems. I've done nothing new this year. I'm glad I shall be in the express stream for mathematics next year.'

I had brought pressure to bear on the teacher responsible for first year mathematics to provide more challenging problems for this pupil. His mathematics teacher, too, had urged that he should be transferred to the second year, but to no avail. The Maths Club, an innovation, had met this pupil's needs initially. The creation of an express stream in mathematics, beginning in the second year, should provide the necessary stimulus. This pupil had spent the first year at the high school doing nothing new in mathematics and rarely meeting any challenging problems. It seemed wasteful of his exceptional talent that he had had no fun in mathematics during his first year at the secondary phase.

The other able pupils at both high schools referred at their interviews to the scarcity of new work (50% at most), but, perhaps because they had not shared the same absorbing interest in mathematics as the outstanding pupils, they appeared reasonably content with the programme. A girl said, 'It is good to do things again because then you get used to doing it'. Yet, when at the end of the school year I told her that she was to be in the express stream for mathematics, she was delighted. She said, 'I'm so glad. I'm surprised because I didn't do as well as I should in the exams – only in the 60s'. So this girl, too, looked forward to a more demanding pace in mathematics.

All the pupils described mathematics as being taught mainly from books. None of the able pupils during their first year at the high school chose mathematics as their favourite subject – or even as a subject of particular interest. Were their needs being met? Their principal aim seemed to have been 'to get the hang of new topics' when these were introduced. Certainly they needed a period for settling in and for adjusting to specialist teaching. But should this have taken a year? Would they have lost interest in mathematics during the first year – and perhaps the habit of work? One of the able pupils said, 'More explanation is given here so I really know what I'm doing'. Another said, 'The teacher keeps us all together. She explains everything first.' A third commented, 'Maths is alright. If I don't understand I keep the textbook at hand to see what the teacher is trying to say. Here we are made to think more.' Whether there was too much explanation, or not enough, the content did not appear to have aroused great interest.

The teaching in the first year of the high schools seemed to be closely geared to textbooks or to a workcard system. Careful explanation by the teacher was followed by the working of examples by the pupils. Although some pupils had said that they were made to think more at the high school, there were no investigations which could have captured the pupils' interest. It did not seem that their needs in problem-solving were being met. I agreed with the adviser who visited these schools on three occasions for observation that there had been no change in the teaching of first year pupils in content or in style. Above all, there was a very long delay in attempting to meet the special needs of the outstanding pupils.

Middle schools age groups 10 to 12

Slow learners	*Able children*

1. Number facts: addition and subtraction, p. 37–39 multiplication p. 38 square numbers p. 39

1.

2. Dice games: addition p. 39 multiplication p. 40 HTU (place value) p. 40

2. Frequency of occurrence of totals of 0 to 12, when each of the four operations is used for the scores on two dice. Comparison of experimental results with tables made using pairs of numbers from the set 1 to 6 ($+ - \times \div$) p. 116

3. Sampling: odds and evens, division by 4, recording according to remainders, p. 40

3. Sampling: recording remainders after division by 2, 3, 4, p. 115

4. Four operations:
   addition p. 41
   subtraction p. 41–42
   multiplication and division p. 42–44
   fractions, addition and subtraction pp. 44–45

4. Four operations using decimals based on body measures p. 116–118
   Fractions: multiplication and division p. 118
   Multiples: patterns from digit sum p. 121–122
   Prime numbers, p. 123–124

5. Scale: square numbers p. 125 cube numbers $\left(\frac{\text{skin area}}{\text{volume}}\right)$ pp. 127–129

6. Containers: capacities/ cross-sections pp. 130–132

7. Variation in areas when perimeter is fixed: rectangles; triangles; greatest and least areas pp. 133–135

Slow learners   *Able children*

8. Area fixed: halving sheets of
   paper. Making shapes with
   identical halves; mirror and
   rotational symmetries
   pp. 135–138
   Shapes with greatest and
   least perimeters.
9. Graphical representation
   and limits pp. 138–152
10. Miscellaneous problems
    pp. 152–155
    The Kaleidoscope: variation
    in number of images with
    change of angle between
    hinged mirrors;
    triangular numbers.

CHAPTER NINE

Some recommendations for teaching mathematics to gifted children of ages 7 to 12

I. Recommendations resulting from my work with gifted children in project schools

Primary school children who are gifted at mathematics require a programme very different from extension work in other textbooks. They need weekly contact with a teacher who is enthusiastic about mathematics – probably the teacher with responsibility for coordinating mathematics through the school.

The children need opportunities for the interchange of ideas, both with the teacher and with their peers, and also for the appraisal of the different solutions they suggest for the problems they are given. They should become accustomed to describing what they are doing and what they have discovered in simple but correct mathematical language – so that other children understand their findings. Some able children prefer to work on their own. Of course they should have some time for private work but it is essential that they should learn to cooperate with their peers at intervals.

If children who are gifted at mathematics are to work at regular intervals with their peers, it may be necessary to have children from a wider age range working together. Younger children are sometimes at a disadvantage within such an organization. Their problems should be kept under observation.

Sometimes able children are handicapped because they do not have easy recall of basic number facts. These children, as well as all the others, require some help in rationalizing their number knowledge.

Teachers should try to provide some sustained investigations for these children to develop as far as they can. It is an advantage for investigations to be as 'open' as possible (see the children's reaction to investigating the areas of triangles with the same perimeter). It is always possible to 'close' an investigation, but never the reverse. Not only the investigations but the teacher's questioning in the course of these should also be as open as possible. These children welcome a challenge and like to be made to think. Whenever material (such as interlocking cubes, identical unit squares, string) would facilitate an investigation, it should be readily available. The children should be encouraged to use material and not to despise it as only for slow learners.

It is important that secondary teachers of mathematics should know what the able children are doing in the fourth year and what their potential is. The best way of achieving this is for the teachers to visit primary schools to see the children in action. The teachers at primary schools should also be able to visit the secondary school to see the continuation of their work.

Teachers may find the following list of activities used with gifted children of ages 7 to 12 useful in their own work.

II. A list of some of the activities used with able children of ages 7 to 12

(Some of the activities used, particularly with the younger children, will be found in the list for slow learners, pp. 54–66.)

1. Dice games

Material: two sets of cards 0 to 12, two dice.

(a) The children play in pairs. Each arranges a set of cards, in number order, face up on the table. They throw the dice in turn, add the scores and turn the card with the matching total face down. The winner is the first to have all his cards face down.

This game is varied by finding (i) the difference between the scores and (ii) the product of the scores.

Each child then makes tables for the numbers 1 to 6 (a) adding pairs of numbers, (b) finding the difference and (c) finding the product. From each table he finds how many times each number occurs in the table (the frequency of occurrence). Later on, include division of pairs of numbers from the set 1 to 6.

(b) The children use all four operations (addition, difference, multiplication, division) on the dice scores at each throw. They turn down all four cards which match the four results (when possible).

(c) Using all four operation tables the children find the frequency of occurrence of each of the scores 0, 1, ... 12. They compare
these frequencies with their experimental results.

2. Place-value game

Material: two place-value sheets; two sets of cards, 0 to 9. This game is
an extension of the game described for slow learners. The children
play in pairs. The two packs of cards are shuffled together and placed
face down between them. Each player in turn takes a card and places
it in either column of his place-value sheet. The game continues until
each player has taken and placed six cards in all, in either column.
The one whose score is nearest to 100 wins. If, at any stage, a player's
score exceeds 100, he automatically loses the game.

3. Some aspects of the four operations

(a) *Long multiplication*. Material: squared paper.

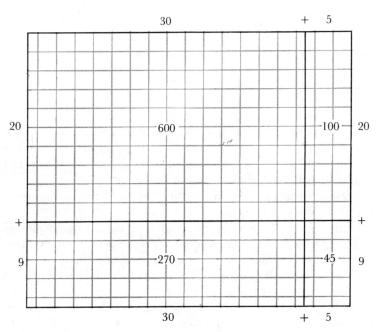

Figure 62

Problem: A classroom is 35 square tiles long and 29 tiles wide. Are there more than 1000 square tiles on the floor? When the children are provided with squared paper they usually think of using one square for one tile and drawing the classroom to scale on the paper. They then divide the classroom up as shown in Figure 62 to make the calculation easier, and find the number of tiles in each section, adding these to find the total. (This is a useful method for any calculation by multiplication.)

(b) *Multiplication of fractions.* Material: squared paper.

Although calculations using decimals are likely to occur more frequently than calculations using fractions, there are occasions when fractions provide a simpler calculation. They are sometimes encountered in area problems. For example, $\frac{1}{2} \times \frac{3}{4}$ can be represented as in Figure 63. Each small square is $\frac{1}{16}$ of the whole square. The shaded area is 6 small squares or $\frac{6}{16}$ of the whole square. So $\frac{1}{2} \times \frac{3}{4} = \frac{6}{16}$, or $\frac{3}{8}$.

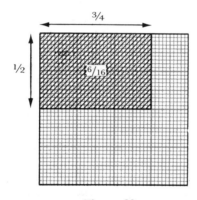

Figure 63

(c) *Division of fractions.*

Even able children require a great deal of experience of this concept before they can solve abstract problems. First revise simple division. How many sets of 3 in 13? In symbols, this is $12 \div 3$, or 4 sets of 3. How many quarter glasses can you pour from a whole glass? In symbols, this is $1 \div \frac{1}{4} = 4$. Also $2 \div \frac{1}{4} = 8$, etc.

How many $1\frac{1}{2}$ cm lengths can be cut from 20 cm of balsa wood?

In symbols, we have to calculate $20 \div 1\frac{1}{2}$.

Working in $\frac{1}{2}$ cm lengths this is: $40 \div 3$ or 13 lengths and 1 ($\frac{1}{2}$ cm) left.

(An eight-year-old girl invented this simple method for dividing fractions!)

   (d) *Decimals – one and two places.*   Material: coloured strips of sugar paper; tape measure; square centimetre paper, scissors.

First extend the place value sequence: $100 \quad 10 \quad 1 \quad \frac{1}{10} \quad \frac{1}{100}$

Show the children the shorthand way of 0.1

writing the fractions in decimal form. $0.0 \quad 1$

Then concentrate on experiences which give practice in using one place of decimals; for example, the children cut paper strips to match their height, reach, and various perimeters such as head, face, foot. After comparing and writing about the strips they measure these, first to the nearest centimetre, then in decimetres (one place of decimals). All four operations can be applied to these lengths (in decimetres, to give practice in using decimals). Ask questions such as: 'Which three of your measures together are nearest to your height? How near is your height to your reach? How many of your feet tall are you? Is twice your neck perimeter longer or shorter than your waist perimeter?'

   Also give practice in using a decimetre strip of centimetre squared paper, one centimetre wide. The children colour a number of squares and then record all the questions they can devise. They circulate these to others for answers. 'How much longer is the coloured section than the uncoloured? What is the total length of coloured and uncoloured sections? How many uncoloured sections are there in the total length? Is twice the coloured section longer than the uncoloured section?' (Vary the total length of the strip.)

   The children also make a tenth scale three-dimensional model of themselves, with strips of centimetre/mm paper, based on their original measured strips. When the work is extended to two places of decimals, the children cut out several square decimetres from centimetre squared paper. Each of the square centimetres is 0.01 of a square decimetre. The square decimetres can be used for short practice sessions – as were the decimetre strips. The children then draw round one of their feet on centimetre squared paper and find its area, first in square centimetres, then in square decimetres. They also cut out an area equal to that of their foot from centimetre squared paper, one decimetre wide (to make super-imposition easy). Working in a group of four, they find the difference between the smallest and the largest foot areas, and the average foot area for the group. (For activities which will help children to acquire the concept of an average see pp. 90–91.) The children can make up their own problems to include all four operations. The answers can be found practically and checked with a calculating machine.

Problems involving money should be included when children are working to two places of decimals.

4. Sampling and averages

Material: small pebbles or other counting material.

The children use the pebbles to take ten random samples, one at a time, and record the remainders when they are dividing by 4 (also by 2, 3, 5, etc.). As a group they find the frequency of occurrence of each remainder, the average of the totals and which number of each remainder is nearest to or farthest from the average.

5. Patterns of digit sums of various multiples

The children write down the multiples of 9 until they 'top' 100. They then add the digits for each multiple until they obtain a single digit. They describe the pattern. They repeat this for multiples of 8 and 10, 7 and 11, 6 and 12, and describe and compare the sequences of digit sums. They also investigate multiples of 3.

6. Prime numbers

Material: unit squares, preferably in one colour.

Using unit squares, for each number, beginning with 1, the children make as many different rectangles (including squares) as they can.

and count as different rectangles for the number 2.

They make a table showing, for each number, the total number of rectangles they can make. They investigate this sequence, paying special attention to the totals for square numbers, and to the set of 2-rectangle numbers.

They make a six-day calendar, ring the prime numbers, and describe their positions in the table.

7. Scale

Materials: unit squares in two colours; interlocking unit cubes.

(a) The children use two handfuls of unit squares to make the largest square they can. (They usually make square frames – but do not reject complete squares.) They investigate and describe different methods of working out the number of unit squares they would need to make a 10 by 10 frame (five methods at least).

(b) They investigate and describe the different methods of building larger and larger squares from unit squares (three methods at least).

(c) They make a shape using a few interlocking cubes. They enlarge the shape (doubling, trebling, quadrupling the dimensions), using interlocking cubes. They investigate relationships between lengths, areas and volumes.

(d) The children make a sequence of enlarging cubes, using inter-locking cubes. They record in a table the edge lengths, base perimeters, base areas, total surface areas, volumes, and the surface area/volume rate, for all the cubes in their sequences. They find the number patterns and make various representations and graphs.

8. Containers of different shapes with the same perimeter

The children investigate (a) the areas of different shapes with the same perimeter, finding the largest possible shape for that perimeter; (b) the areas of rectangle with this perimeter; (c) the areas of triangles with this perimeter.

9. Miscellaneous problems

(a) They investigate the perimeters of rectangles (and other shapes) with the same area.

(b) They investigate the number of reflections (plus the object) which they see in hinged mirrors when the angle between the mirrors is changed.

(c) The children investigate triangular numbers.

10. Generalization

On every possible occasion I encouraged the children to generalize their findings. For example, when they were suggesting methods for finding the number of unit squares used for making larger and larger square frames, some children gradually began to express their sugges-tions in symbolic form. They used algebra to express their solutions.

11. Limits

When the children made graphical representations of the results of their investigations (for example, of the widths and lengths of rectangles with the same area), I asked them to describe the effect of making the width as short as possible. They took the width to be 0.1 cm, 0.01 cm, and so on, and calculated the corresponding lengths of the rectangles. They appreciated that the graph showing the widths and lengths of the set of rectangles would never quite meet the axis. In this way the concept of a limit was developed. The section which follows explains the mathematical background of the various graphs made by the children.

III. A summary of the mathematical background of the graphs made by the able children at the middle schools

A. Multiplication tables

(1) Block graphs using interlocking cubes (the representation for each table has equal steps).

(2) Straight line graphs, for example, $y = x$, $y = 2x$, $y = 3x$. These are graphs of constant ratio: $y/x = 1$, $y/x = 2$, $y/x = 3$, etc.

(3) Line graphs of the perimeters of enlarging squares. (The perimeters are often cut from string first and attached to the corresponding square.) This graph is $y = 4x$.

All these graphs represent 'direct proportion'. (Another example of direct proportion is cost. For instance, the cost of two or more gallons of petrol at 197 pence a gallon.) The characteristic of direct propor-

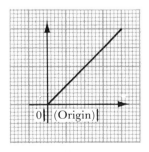

Figure 64

tion is that when x is doubled, y is doubled, when x is trebled, y is trebled. (We pay twice as much for two gallons of petrol.) All line graphs illustrating direct proportion are straight lines passing through the origin (Figure 64).

B. Areas of squares with edge lengths in whole numbers

These areas are represented:

(1) as a number pattern (with odd number differences, in order);

(2) as a block graph made from strips, one unit wide, cut from each square in turn (Figure 65 and 45). The steps are unequal and increasing, but form a pattern (the odd numbers: 1, 3, 5, 7 ....).

(3) as a line graph, $y = x^2$. This is a curve (see Figure 46, page 141).

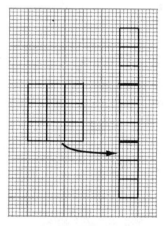

Figure 65

C. Volumes of cubes

Material: interlocking cubes.

These volumes are represented

(1) as a number pattern which can be recognized after taking the second differences;

(2) as a block graph made from the interlocking cubes which form each cube in the sequence. The steps are unequal and increasing: 1, 7, 19, 37,61, 91, ... (The second differences are 6, 12, 18, 24, 30 .....) The line graph, $y = x^3$, is a curve (see Figure 46, page 141).

D. The constant product relationship: inverse proportion

Example (1)   The widths and lengths of rectangles with the same area.

(1) Number pattern.

width (cm)	1	2	3	4	6	9	12	18	36
length (cm)	36	18	12	9	6	4	3	2	1

(We could of course use intermediate values for the width.)
Characteristic of inverse proportion: when the width is doubled, the length is halved; when the width is trebled, the length is 'thridded'.

(2) The line graph of $xy = 36$ is a curve (Figure 57 page 151). The mirror line is $y = x$.

(3) A 'block' graph can be made by cutting out the complete set of rectangles in (1), and then overlapping these as far as possible (Figure 56 page 150).

(4) The same pattern can be seen in the multiplication square (ringed and hatched squares, Table 24 page 149). These are number pairs whose product is 36.

Example (2)   The number pairs obtained by changing the angle between hinged mirrors and recording the number of reflections (plus object) seen in the mirrors for different angles have a similar pattern. Since recordings are made only when there is a whole number of reflections, the points should not be joined to make a curved line. (Try the experiment if it is new to you, and complete the table. Check that it represents an inverse relationship and find the constant product.)

Table 26

Angle between mirrors	No. of images plus one
180°	2
120°	3
90°	4

All these graphs belong to the same 'family'.
This family resembles our counting system:

.... 1000   100   10   1 $\frac{1}{10}$ $\frac{1}{100}$ $\frac{1}{1000}$ ....

Each successive term is obtained by dividing the previous term by 10.
Another way of writing this sequence is:

$$10 \times 10 \times 10 \quad 10 \times 10 \quad 10 \quad 1 \quad \frac{1}{10} \quad \frac{1}{10 \times 10} \quad \frac{1}{10 \times 10 \times 10}$$

This sequence can also be re-written:

$$10^3 \qquad 10^2 \quad 10^1 \; 10^0 \quad 10^{-1} \quad 10^{-2} \qquad 10^{-3}$$

Our family is therefore:

x^3	x^2	x^1	x^0	x^{-1}
(cubes of numbers)	(squares)	straight lines of direct proportion)	or 1	(graphs of inverse proportion or constant product)

All these relationships are already familiar to us, except $y = 1$. $y = 1$ for *all* values of x, therefore its graph is as in Figure 66. We occasionally come across examples of this relationship: for example, if we were to take ground temperatures throughout the day and the temperature remained the same all day.

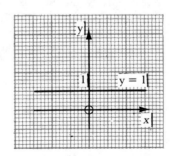

Figure 66

E. Constant sum

Material: squared paper, scissors.

Example: Rectangles with the same perimeter: e.g. 20 cm. The sum of the width and length is always 10 cm.

(1) The number pattern is shown in Table 21, page 145. The relationship is $x + y = 10$.

(2) If the set of rectangles in Table 21 is cut out and overlapped as far as possible, Figure 50, page 145 is obtained. This can be compared with the line of shaded squares in Table 22, page 146. These contain number pairs whose sum is 10.

(3) The line graph of the number pairs which satisfy (fit the equation $x + y = 10$) is shown in Figure 51, page 147.

F. Areas of rectangles with the same perimeter (20 cm)

(1) Figure 21, page 103 shows that the areas decrease by the 'odd number pattern'. (What would be the pattern for arcas of rectangles with perimeter 22 cm?)

(2) A block graph of the areas was made by cutting each rectangle in the sequence into strips 1 cm wide (Figure 52, page 147.)

(3) The relationship for the areas of the set of rectangles can be found. Width x cm, y cm is the length. Perimeter 20 cm.

$\therefore$ $x + y = 10$, so that $y = 10 - x$.

The area A of the rectangles is xy or $x (10 - x)$.

The line graph of $A = x (10 - x)$ is shown in Figure 53, page 148.

Since this number pattern is decreasing odd numbers (from 9), and the difference pattern of the square numbers is the odd numbers increasing from 1, it is not surprising that the graph of the areas of rectangles with the same perimeter is the reverse (turned upside down) of the graph of the square numbers (if squares of negative numbers are included). Donald at Missingham made this comparison (Figure 67 next page).

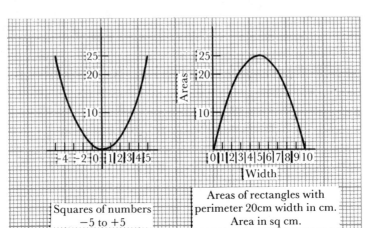

Figure 67

CHAPTER TEN

Other investigations and other children

I. Introduction

The three pieces of work described in this chapter were each started by a small group of very able children during their fourth year at a junior school. In the first two examples the whole class became closely involved with the problem. (There were 80 children in the fourth year, of whom 48 were in the A class.) Every child not only made his own personal contribution but was able to talk, with complete understanding, about what the class had discovered by working as a team. An attractive and detailed class record was made of the development of both investigations, which ultimately included other aspects of the curriculum.

The teacher of this fourth year class was an experienced and imaginative teacher of mathematics (and of everything else). She had a good mathematical background and was relaxed and confident in her teaching. She welcomed the children's suggestions, and encouraged them to develop these in their own way when they were engaged on a sustained investigation. They caught her enthusiasm for mathematics and worked for long periods at this subject. The recordings of their discoveries always included a written account, numerical tables and graphs, and they often chose to paint pictures to illustrate what they were doing.

II. The first investigation

The first extensive investigation developed from a project on the strengths of structures. I had asked the teacher to see how the children responded to this problem:

Using cardboard strips and paper-fasteners make shapes with 3, 4, 5 .... sides. Find the least number of strips you have to add to make each frame rigid. When the frame is rigid, what do you notice about the shape of the component parts? Record your results like this:

Number of sides	Number of triangles
3	1
4	2
:	:

Find the sum of the angles of regular frames with 3, 4, 5, ... sides, giving your answers in right angles. Represent your results on a graph.

Finally, the children were asked to find the angles of regular frames with 3, 4, ... to 12 sides and to graph the results. 'Do they represent a law?' was the final question[1].

The children found that both of the first two graphs were straight lines. (They concluded that these graphs represented a law.) They found the angles of the regular polygons from the sum of the angles (in degrees). For example, the sum of the angles of the hexagon was 4×2 right angles or $720°$ (since the four triangles they made with struts included all the angles of the hexagon). Since the hexagon was regular, each angle was $720° \div 6$, or $120°$ (Figure 68).

Here is part of the letter written to me by the two boys who began work on the project:

When you came to our school, you talked about graphs. You demonstrated, by throwing a piece of chalk into the air, that whatever goes up must come down[2]. (Michael and I understood that this principle applied to a curved graph).

---

[1] You will notice that at that time (1960) I left nothing to chance. My questions were directed to enabling children, step by step, to make the discoveries I had in mind. They were shown how to tabulate their results and asked to represent these on graphs. It was later on that I gradually came to appreciate the advantages of asking more flexible questions so that the children could develop investigations in their own way. But the directed start did not inhibit the children. They went on to make other discoveries – far beyond the original limits I set them.

[2] I had been showing the children that the graph they had drawn of the area of rectangles with the same perimeter closely resembled that of the path of an object thrown through the air.

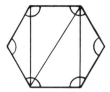

Figure 68

The two boys calculated the angles of regular polygons with 3, 4, ... 12 sides and made a graph of their results. The letter continued:

> The graph turned out to be in a curve, so Michael and I decided to see if there was a turning point [as in the graph they had made before]. This graph was of extra interest because if we could reach 180° we should have come to a figure supposedly made of straight lines.

At this point the teacher was absent from school for some time. The two boys told the head that they had a problem they wanted to solve and that they would involve everyone in the class to help in the calculations. (In those days there were no electronic calculating machines!) They explained the problem to the class and organized the children in groups. Each group knew the calculations for which its members were responsible. The letter continued:

> We are enclosing the graph which we plotted up to 240 sides and then discontinued as it looked as though it would go on for ever. We jumped in tens, fifties, hundreds, five hundreds, thousands, hundred thousands, and finally millions in our effort to reach 180°. We could have saved ourselves some work if we had noticed the pattern earlier, e.g.:

100	sides	angles	176.4
1000			179.64
10,000			179.964
100,000			179.9964
1,000,000			179.99964
10,000,000			179.999964
100,000,000			179.9999964

They also included the angles for polygons with 240, 2400, etc., sides. 'When we noticed this pattern we realized that we never should reach 180° or turn the graph. On May 11th at 10.15 a.m. we finally gave in.' (The last entry was 450 million sides.)

Before this letter reached me the head of the school telephoned me to ask for my help. She said, 'Mrs. X is still away. The children are very excited. I know they've made a discovery, but I'm afraid I shall not understand what it is.'

By the time I was able to visit the school the teacher had returned. Excitement ran very high. The classroom walls were covered with a wide variety of paintings. Not surprisingly, the dominating theme was polygons – of all shapes and sizes.

The teacher asked some of the quieter and the slower children to tell me about their part in the investigation and to show me their calculations. It was evident that every child in the class was eager to talk about the initial problem and what they had discovered. They had been carried along by the enthusiasm of George and Michael and had been undaunted by the magnitude of the calculations which they had carried out. The teacher and I were as excited as the children.

The children's letter had concluded: 'We think this is the most exciting piece of maths we have ever done. It is just like research work.'

The investigation was indeed of research standard. These children had a firm grasp of the concept of a mathematical limit, more so than many students at universities without first hand experience.

The investigation did not end here. While the children were calculating the interior angles of various regular polygons they became aware of the correspondingly decreasing sizes of the exterior angles. For example, a polygon of 100 sides had an interior angle of 176.4° and therefore an exterior angle of 3.6°; a polygon with 1000 sides had an interior angle of 179.64° and an exterior angle of 0.36°. These observations led the children first to make a table showing the interior and exterior angles of the regular polygons they had originally studied, and then to represent both sets of results by two lines on the same axes.

I asked them if they were justified in joining the points to make continuous lines. 'Do the intermediate points on your lines have a meaning?', I asked. My question made them realize that they did not. But they said, 'We wanted to know whether the line was a smooth curve or not; that would tell us whether there was a law'.

No. of sides	interior angles	exterior angles
3	60°	120°
4	90°	90°
5	108°	72°
6	120°	60°

They continued the table to polygons of 12 sides. The symmetry of the two lines intrigued the children and they inserted the line of symmetry on the graph where the two curves met, where the interior and exterior angles were the same (90°) (Figure 69).

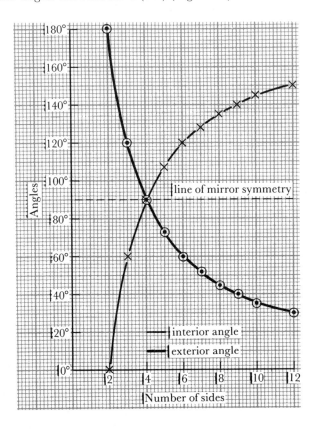

Figure 69: Angles (interior and exterior) of regular shapes

Another stage of the investigation followed work done by the
children on the areas of circles, in their effort to find the largest area
that could be enclosed by a given length of string. Their attention
became focused on the perimeters and areas of ellipses. By this time
George and Michael were working with Philip and Susan. I found the
group struggling to construct points on an ellipse, using two drawing
pins and identical loops of string (on squared paper). Each time the
string was passed round two fixed points marked by drawing pins, the
string was pulled taut using a pencil, and the point was marked. The
children tried to space the points equally round the perimeter. They
asked me if there was an easier method of constructing points on an
ellipse. When I suggested that compasses might help if they used the
two foci (fixed points on the axis) as centres, they soon discovered that
all they had to do was to make sure that AP + PB (the loop of string)
remained the same length (Figure 70).

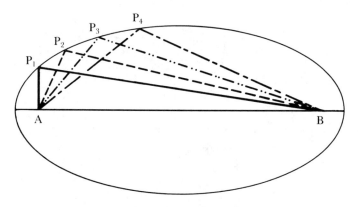

Figure 70

They had calculated the approximate area of each ellipse they constructed. They asked, 'Is there a formula for the area of an ellipse so
that we can check our counting method?'. I explained that the area of
an ellipse was related to that of a circle. 'How do you know that the
ellipse and the circle are related to each other?', I asked. George
replied, 'When you draw a set of ellipses with the same loop of string,
gradually moving the drawing pins closer together each time, you end
up with both drawing pins together at the centre. The shape is then a
circle.' Michael continued, 'The area of a circle of radius r is πr^2. If the

half axes (shortest and longest 'radii' of the ellipse) are *a* and *b*, is its area *πab?* When *a* and *b* are each *r* that would make the area of a circle *πr*²'. I congratulated the group on their intuition.

Then they asked me about their other problem: the formula for the perimeter of the ellipse, which they had measured by using string. I explained that I had not come across this formula until my third year at university and that it was too complex for them to understand at present. Disappointed, but undaunted, they decided to use *π* (*a* + *b*) for the perimeter of an ellipse instead of 2*πr* as for a circle. They compared their experimental results, using string, with their calculations using the formula they had invented. It was a useful approximation, but at the end of the summer term, just before they left school, the group wrote:

> We were not successful in finding the formula for the circumference (of an ellipse) but we were able to prove [check?] the formula for the area. The circumference graph has not made a perfectly straight line – which is worrying us ....
> For us this has been a very exciting maths year. The part I have enjoyed most is trying to find things for myself and Michael and Philip say the same.

What a wonderful testimony this letter is to the contribution that mathematics can make to the primary school curriculum, when children are helped and encouraged by their teacher to experiment for themselves and to make their own personal contribution. Moreover, their enthusiasm can affect other children in their year and can help them to achieve mathematics far in advance of the usual work undertaken at this stage.

III. The second project

The second major project, undertaken by a subsequent fourth year class in the same school, followed an investigation called 'Gulliver's mathematics'. The children constructed a six-foot tall model of Gulliver and beside him they placed Lilliputians, also made full-scale. In *Gulliver's Travels* they had read that after the Lilliputians had tied Gulliver down and realized how big he was, they brought him food far in excess of his needs. This discovery prompted an enquiry (which came to be called 'Mouse and Man') into the average daily weight of food required by various creatures, including humans, to maintain their energy. As in the first investigation, the enquiry was started by a group of able children but enthusiasm spread and all the class became involved.

The study began by the children weighing Jane's mouse and finding the average amount of food the mouse ate in one day. They found that a one-ounce mouse ate, on average, half an ounce of food in one day. Just before this experiment was carried out, a boy in the class acquired a new baby brother. He proudly reported to the class that his brother, who weighed eight pounds, had six feeds a day of five ounces. 'That's nearly one quarter of his weight', Mark said. Jane then remembered what she had read on a packet of bird seed, 'A blackbird needs one quarter of its weight in food daily'.

At this point some of the children decided to weigh the food they ate each day for a week. They found that they ate about 1/25 of their weight in food every day. Finally, they persuaded their fathers to take part in the experiment. They found that these adults ate about 1/50 of their weight daily.

In the class discussion which followed, attention was focused on why we need to have regular meals during the day. Some children said that they required food in order to grow – but why did adults need to eat? How else did we use our energy and need to replenish it? Mark suggested that we run about and get hot, then we sweat and get cool again. This suggestion directed attention to one of the functions of the skin. So the next experiment was to compare ten-year-old Alison's skin area with her weight, and Jane's mouse's skin area with its weight. The children recorded:

Alison and Mouse

Total surface area of Alison = 1748 square inches
weight = 6 st. 5 lb.
Mouse: we made a clay mouse of the size of Jane's and marked it in ¼ sq. ins.

surface area = 23 quarter sq. ins.
Weight of real mouse = 1 ounce

$$\frac{\text{Surface area}}{\text{weight}} \text{for Alison} = \frac{1748}{89} \left[\begin{array}{l} \times 4 \rightarrow \text{quarter sq. ins.} \\ \times 16 \rightarrow \text{ozs} \end{array} = \frac{1}{4} \right]$$

$$= 5 \text{ to } 1$$

for mouse = 23 to 1

This proves that the mouse has a surface area almost five times bigger in comparison to its weight or volume than has Alison. The mouse has more area to lose heat from than man by comparison – so has to eat more by comparison than man to replace it.

The teacher then suggested that the children should find out what happens to the $\dfrac{\text{surface area}}{\text{volume}}$ of a mathematical shape as it is enlarged, since Alison and the mouse were so different in shape (as well as size). They decided to use unit cubes to make a sequence of larger cubes, and to compare the surface area and volume of each. (One boy enlarged coloured rods instead 'because my father isn't a cube'.)
Here is the beginning of the table they made.

Surface and volume

Side	Area of one face	Area of six faces	Volume
1	$1^2 = 1$ square unit	6 sq. units	1
2	$2^2 = 4$ square units	24 sq. units	8
:	: :		
10	$10^2 = 100$ square units	600 sq. units	1000

They represented these results on one graph (Figure 71) which they described in this way:

Graphs of cubes (Figure 71). The surface area and volume of six faces. These graphs show that the figures for surface area are greater than those for volume for small cubes (up to a side of 6 units) and smaller than those for volume for large cubes.

This investigation then developed in different ways:

(i) Alison recorded: 'At school we decided to find out how much air pressure at 15 lb. per square inch was pressing on me.

My surface area = 1748 sq. ins.
Weight of air on me = 1748 × 15 lb.
= 11.7 tons'

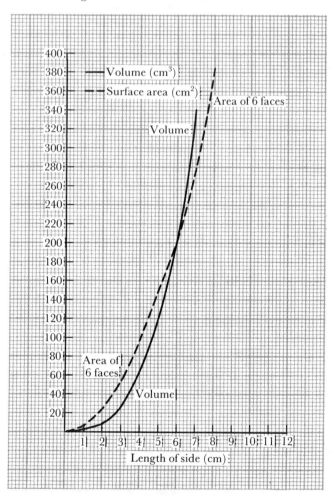

Figure 71

'How do you manage to carry so much weight about?' Alison was asked by a younger child.

(ii) The children read in a book that air pressure falls with increasing height above sea level. They made a graph to show the pressure in pounds per square inch at different heights above sea level. They also read in Sir John Hunt's *Ascent of Everest* that at high altitude the cooking of meat, rice and vegetables is extremely slow because water boils at a lower temperature than at sea level. They next made a graph showing how the boiling point of water changed with differing air pressure. To develop this concept the teacher suggested that every child should choose a high mountain anywhere in the world, locate the mountain on a world map and record its height. They then read the air pressure at that height from their first graph and read the boiling point of water at that pressure from the second graph. All the children recorded their results in the class book of mountains, summits, air pressure and boiling point of water. One boy's record read: 'Sierra Nevada: 11,420 ft. – two miles up. Air pressure at summit 9½ lb per square inch. Boiling point of water 89°C.'

This project continued for a long period. It had started with a mathematical problem but eventually included other aspects of the curriculum, particularly geography and science.

IV. The third investigation

The third investigation was different from the others partly because attention was focused on mathematics throughout, and because this enquiry continued for six months. Moreover, the boy who started it was so anxious to find a solution that, as he said, 'I worked at my problem every night except Sundays and scout nights'.

The enquiry began in November 1963. Peter was a member of a class of over 40 ten-year-olds who, until September 1963, had followed a traditional scheme in arithmetic. The fourth year teacher who took them over had by now equipped a mathematics room with attractive problems and the materials required to solve them. She first introduced the class to the mathematics room, suggesting that they should work with two or three friends on any problem in the room which interested them. They toured the problems, then congregated defensively in the middle of the room, saying, 'We like arithmetic'. The teacher, realizing their apprehension about the new way of working, changed her tactics. For a time she used the new topics she planned to cover, with the class as a whole. The new topics included: graphs of the multiplication tables (Figure 72, page 190), squares (their perimeters and areas), triangular numbers and their relationship with square numbers, cubes (the perimeters and areas of their bases, and their volumes), mathematical gradients and ratios. Throughout, the teacher stressed the importance of discovering patterns and describing these. On the first day she had said, 'In mathematics, there's always a pattern – you've only got to look for it'.

After a while, some of the children began to take an interest in the original problems. Peter was one of these. He and two friends worked with a truck running down rails fixed to a long plank. They propped one end of the plank first on one brick, then on two bricks, and so on. Each time, they used a stop watch to find how long the truck took to run down the slope. After a few experiments Peter asked the teacher, 'If we time the truck when the plank is propped first on one brick, then on two, will the second time be half the first?'. The teacher answered, 'I don't know, Peter. Why don't you try the experiment yourself?' This was the first piece of independent work Peter had undertaken. It took him the whole morning to find the answer to his question.

Sometime later on (in November) Peter said to the teacher, 'I hope you won't mind. I don't want to solve any more of your problems, because I've got a problem of my own.' He then referred to the graph of $y = x^2$ which he had drawn as part of the class work (Figure 73). He

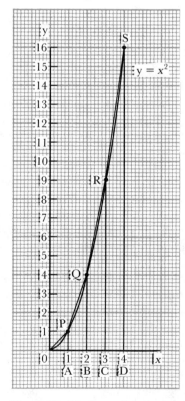

Figure 73: Mathematics–Angles

continued: 'I've drawn the gradients at different points on the curve. I can see that the gradients are changing all the time and I want to find the pattern.' Before the teacher could reply Peter continued, 'And the areas under the curve are changing, too. I want to find that pattern as well.' The teacher was very surprised and enquired, 'But what makes you think that there *is* a pattern, Peter?'. He replied at once, 'On the first day you told us that in mathematics there's always a pattern – you've only got to look for it'.

Peter's graph looked like Figure 73. He had marked points on the curve $y = x^2$ at equal intervals of x, i.e. at $x = 1$ (P), $x = 2$ (Q), $x = 3$

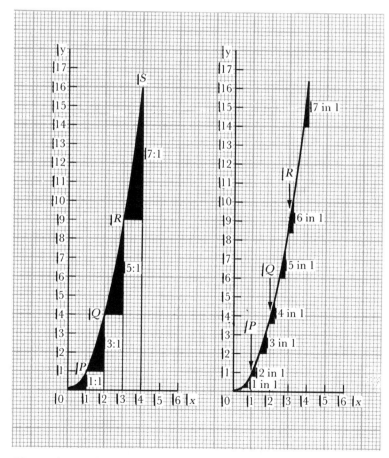

Figures 74 and 75: Mathematical gradients (tables of squares) $y = x^2$)

(R) and so on. When he joined OP, PQ, QR, RS, he had noticed that the slopes of these lines (their gradients) were changing. He had also noticed that the areas OPA, APQB, BQRC, etc., were changing. He wanted to find the patterns of change in each case.

In mathematics the slope or gradient at each point of a curve is actually measured by the slope of the tangent at that point, i.e. the line which touches the curve at that point but does not cut the curve. Peter intuitively included these tangents when he drew 'small triangles' at P, Q, R, etc. (Figure 75).

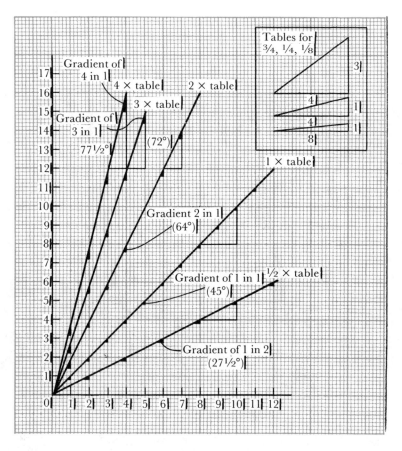

Figure 72: Mathematics – Angles

When the teacher asked Peter whether he wanted to work on his own at his problem, he answered, 'I'm not all that good at spotting patterns – so I'd like to work with my friends'.

Peter and his two friends used practical methods, of course, to solve these problems – as did Archimedes who had solved the same problems more than 2000 years earlier. Peter found the pattern of the mathematical* gradients (changing as x increased) by making careful drawings of triangles and by measurement. He found, by counting squares, the pattern of the areas under curves as x increased. (Archimedes is said to have found this pattern by weighing successive sections of the areas under the curve.) Neither Peter nor Archimedes was afraid of taking intuitive leaps when they were searching for patterns.

Peter worked on both problems simultaneously. He began on the first problem by finding the mathematical gradients of the multiplication tables (Figure 72.) You will see that he checked that the gradient was the same at different points on each line by drawing many small triangles. He measured the angle of elevation (slope) of each line to the horizontal (the x axis).

He then focused attention on the changing gradients of the curve $y = x^2$ (Figure 74 and Figure 75). He began by finding the gradients (in the form of ratios) for each section made by drawing a 'triangle' with each successive unit of x as base (Figure 74). The table he made (Table 27) shows that he had now discovered the pattern of the increasing gradients for each section.

---

* Peter always referred to the gradients as mathematical gradients. Some time earlier the class had carried out a project on gradients of hills in the UK. Gradients of hills are measured 'up the slope', i.e. a 1 in 4 slope is a vertical rise of 1 unit for 4 units up the road. A mathematical gradient of 1 in 4 is a rise of 1 unit vertically for 4 units horizontally.

Hill gradient of 1 in 4   Mathematical gradient of 1 in 4

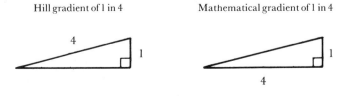

Table 27: $y = x^2$

Section			Piece of y	Piece of x	Approximate area of 'triangle'*	Gradient
From	0,0	to 1,1	1	1	$12\frac{1}{2}$ sm. sq. units	1 in 1
From	1,1	to 2,4	3	1	$37\frac{1}{2}$ sm. sq. units	3 in 1
From	2,4	to 3,9	5	1	$62\frac{1}{2}$ sm. sq. units	5 in 1
	. . .					
	. . .					
From	10,100	to 11,121	21	1	$262\frac{1}{2}$ sm. sq. units	21 in 1

* 'These are not really triangles because one side is curved.'

Peter wrote: 'The gradient increases by two in the odd numbers so that the gradient = 1 in 1, 3 in 1, 5 in 1, etc.' He then made Table 28.

Table 28

x	1		2		3		4	
SLOPE	1 in 1	2 in 1	3 in 1	4 in 1	5 in 1	6 in 1	7 in 1	8 in 1

[and so on to $x = 6$]

Peter continued:

What I wanted to find was the slope at the points $(1,1)$, $(2,4)$, $(3,9)$, $(4,16)$ ... which was between the 'triangles' I had used before for the slopes of 1 in 1, 3 in 1, 5 in 1, and 7 in 1. I drew small triangles at these points which was the best way I could find it (Figure 75). I found the slopes which are shown in Table 28. The slope is twice the value of x. Slope = $2x$.

The next curve for which Peter found the pattern of the changing gradients was $y = x^3$. He followed the same method, first finding the pattern of the slopes of different sections of the graph, using consecutive units of x (Figure 76). Once more he wrote: 'I supposed that the slope was a series of straight lines'.

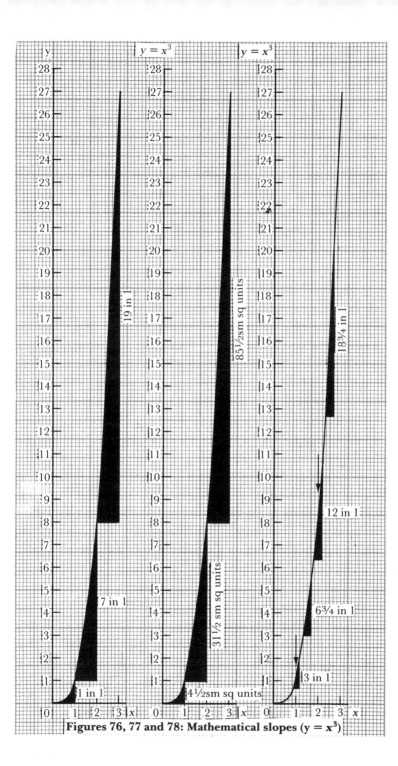

Figures 76, 77 and 78: Mathematical slopes ($y = x^3$)

Table 29: $y = x^3$

Section	Piece of y	Piece of x	Area of triangle	Gradient
From 0,0 to 1,1	1	1	$4\frac{1}{2}$ sm. sq. units	1 in 1
From 1,1 to 2,8	7	1	$31\frac{1}{2}$ sm. sq. units	7 in 1
From 2,8 to 3,27	19	1	$85\frac{1}{2}$ sm. sq. units	19 in 1
From 3,27 to 4,64	37	1	$166\frac{1}{2}$ sm. sq. units	37 in 1
and so on to				
10,1000 to 11,1331	331	1	$1488\frac{1}{2}$ sm. sq. units	331 in 1

He found the pattern of the gradients but omitted to include a table. He wrote: 'To find the gradient at the different points on the graph you square the number at x and multiply by three, i.e. $3^2 = 9$ and $9 \times 3 = 27$ ∴ the gradient at (3,27) is 27 in 1'. Later on, Peter expressed the gradient as $3x^2$, Figure 78.

Peter also used triangles to solve his second problem: the pattern of the areas changing as x increases under the curve $y = x^2$. He first noticed from Figure 74 and Table 27 that the areas of the 'sectional triangles' were increasing in a pattern. He wrote:

> The area of the 'triangles' goes up by 25 small square units for each triangle. The height of the 'triangle' increases by two large units, each time, each one having an area of 25 small square units. (∴ to find the area of each triangle: $50 \div 2 = 25$.)

Table 29 column 4 shows the areas under the curve $y = x^3$ (found, as before, from the areas of triangles, Figure 77). Peter recorded:

Table 30

(Figure 77) Areas of triangles	$4\frac{1}{2}$		$31\frac{1}{2}$		$85\frac{1}{2}$		$166\frac{1}{2}$		$274\frac{1}{2}$		$409\frac{1}{2}$
First differences		27		54		81		108		135	
Differences of differences			27		27		27		27		

The figures above (Table 30) show that when the 'triangle' areas are written down and the differences of the differences are written down all the numbers come to 27. To find the areas between different points in small square units you add:

27	2×27	3×27	4×27	5×27
(27)	(54)	(81)	(108)	(135)

Table 31: Areas beneath curve* (Figures 79 and 80)

$A = \frac{8\frac{1}{2}}{25} = \frac{1}{3}$ square units approx.

$B = 1 + \frac{33}{25} = 2\frac{8}{25} = 2\frac{1}{3}$ sq. units approx. $\qquad A + B = 2\frac{1}{3} + \frac{1}{3} = 2\frac{2}{3}$

$C = 6\,\frac{8\frac{1}{2}}{25} = 6\frac{1}{3}$ square units approx. $\qquad A + B + C = \frac{1}{3} + 2\frac{1}{3} + 6\frac{1}{3} = 9$

$D = 12\frac{1}{3}$ square units approx. $\qquad A + B + C + D = 21\frac{1}{3}$

* This refers to the total area of each section between the curve and the baseline.

You will notice (from the right hand sides of Tables 31 and 32 that Peter had by then decided to find the cumulative areas, i.e. A, A+B, A+B+C, A+B+C+D. He then made Table 32 to show this new development.

Table 32

	Area between	Area	Area between	Area
by experiment	A) $x = 0$ and $x = 1$	$\frac{1}{3}$ sq. unit	$x = 0, x = 1$	$\frac{1}{3}$
	B) $x = 1$ and $x = 2$	$2\frac{1}{3}$ sq. units	$x = 0, x = 2$	$2\frac{2}{3}$
	C) $x = 2$ and $x = 3$	$6\frac{1}{3}$ sq. units	$x = 0, x = 3$	9
	D) $x = 3$ and $x = 4$	$12\frac{1}{3}$ sq. units	$x = 0, x = 4$	$21\frac{1}{3}$
by pattern	$x = 4$ and $x = 5$	$20\frac{1}{3}$ sq. units	$x = 0, x = 5$	$41\frac{2}{3}$
	$x = 5$ and $x = 6$	$30\frac{1}{3}$ sq. units	$x = 0, x = 6$	72
	$x = 6$ and $x = 7$	$42\frac{1}{3}$ sq. units	$x = 0, x = 7$	$114\frac{1}{3}$

			Pattern			
Area	$\frac{1}{3}$		$2\frac{1}{3}$		$6\frac{1}{3}$	$12\frac{1}{3}$	$20\frac{1}{3}$
Increase		2		4		6	8

The last line of this record shows that Peter had succeeded in finding that there was a pattern in the sequence of areas under the curve.

When I visited the school to see Peter's work for the first time, he told me, 'This pattern was a hard one to find. It held me up for two days – until I suddenly thought of multiplying the area sequence by 3. Then I saw the area pattern at once.' The teacher said that Peter was wildly excited after he had decided to multiply by 3 and found the pattern. He shouted, 'I've got it. It's x cubed over 3.'

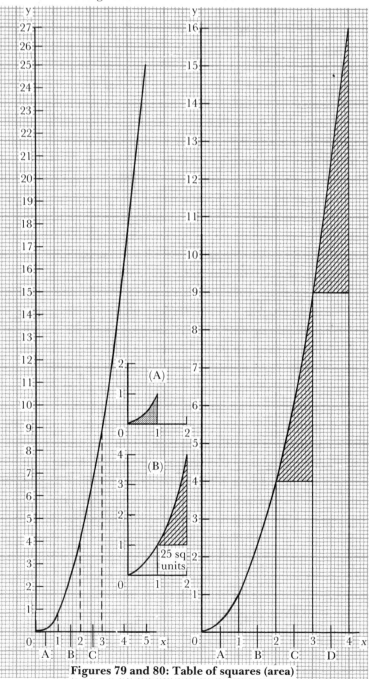

Figures 79 and 80: Table of squares (area)

Here is his recording of this discovery.

Areas from table of squares
Area finishes at $x = 1$ 2   3   4   5
Area $\times$ 3   1   8   27   64   125
These are the cubes of the x numbers.
Area is the x number cubed then divided by 3. Area $= \dfrac{x^3}{3}$

Facts that I know: Graph $y = x^2$
                                    Slope $= 2x$
                                    Area $= \dfrac{x^3}{3}$

After discussing Peter's work with him (with great appreciation) I asked him if he had yet investigated the patterns of the gradients and areas for the graph which preceded $y = x^2$. He wrote: $y = x^3$, $y = x^2$, $y = x^1$, and then worked with $y = x$. He recorded this work (Figure 81):

The graph shows the $y = x$ graph. This is also the $1 \times$ table graph. To find the area square the number at x and half [sic] the total, i.e.
$6 \times 6 = 36$ $36 \div 2 = 18$ Area $= 18$ square units
$$= \frac{x^2}{2}$$

Facts that I know: Graph $y = x$
                                    Slope   1
                                    Area $\dfrac{x^2}{2}$

Peter's account became more highly organized as he continued to work on the problems in which he had such an absorbing interest. He made a careful summary of what his group had achieved. He wrote, 'If I put together all I know this is what it is:

Graph	$y = x$	$y = x^2$	$y = x^3$
Slope	1*	$2x$*	$3x^2$**
Area	$\dfrac{x^2}{2}$*	$\dfrac{x^3}{2}$*	$\dfrac{x^4}{4}$

I found those marked *. Trevor and I found the one marked ** (He saw it from the pattern and we proved it with long length graph paper.) I wrote down $\dfrac{x^4}{4}$ because it follows the pattern of the other areas.'

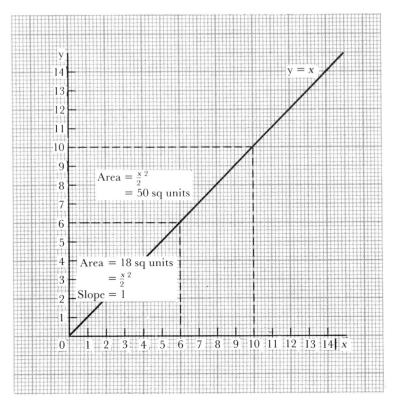

Figure 81: Graph of y = x

Peter made other discoveries while he was searching for the patterns of gradients and areas.

(1) He frequently supported his measurement of gradients and calculations of areas by using more convenient scales on the y axis than those he had begun with (equal scales for x and y).

(2) He became interested in mathematical limits. For example, while he was drawing right-angled triangles with different gradients he wrote, 'I have drawn two triangles each of which have very stiff slopes, for the angles of elevation are nearly 90° and the top nearly 0°. Is it possible to make the top angle 0°? I don't think so, for if it were possible the line of slope and the opposite line would be in one and be vertical which would not be a slope. A triangle could be 1,000,000 in 1 and the angle could be 89.9999999° but it could never be 90°.'

Towards the end of Peter's 'private work' he explored the relationship between the area of the six faces of a cube ($6x^2$) and its volume (x^3). He drew the graph of $y = \frac{A}{V}$ (Figure 82). He recorded:

The larger the cube, the nearer the graph line will be to $y = 0$. [For] a 12-inch cube the Area over Volume will be .5 $[\frac{6}{12}]$. After I had used these large numbers I saw that $y = \frac{6x^2}{x^3}$ which is $\frac{6}{x}$ and to find $\frac{A}{V}$ all I had to do was to divide the side into 6.

For the side of 1 million inches $y = \dfrac{6}{1,000,000}$ or .000,006.

This shows that however big the number of sides [the length of the side of the cube] the line will never meet the x axis.

[Also] A side could be as small as $\dfrac{1}{1,000,000}$ thus making

$$y = \left| \frac{6}{\dfrac{1}{1,000,000}} \right.$$

which = 6,000,000 and so on. The line will never meet the y axis.

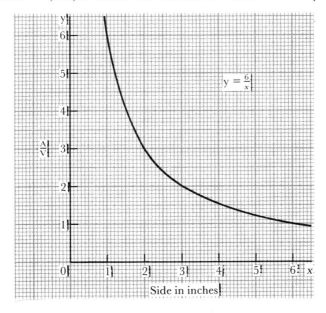

Figure 82: Graph of $\frac{A}{V}$

I have reported the work of Peter and his team at length for several reasons.

(1) Peter's IQ had been assessed as 112. With this IQ in his area Peter would not have gone to a grammar school at that time. But his teacher was so impressed by his achievement that she took his 'private work' to the local education authority. Through her persistence and with the support of the LEA, an illustrated tape-recording was made with Peter discussing his work. In consequence, he was accepted by a grammar school but he found the traditional mathematics course dull and transferred his intense interest in mathematics to physics, in which he was given greater scope for private investigation.

(2) Peter did not reveal his great interest in mathematics until he was encouraged by the teacher to undertake investigations. His extraordinary talent for mathematics could have been missed altogether if he had not been given this opportunity.

(3) Peter's major discoveries depended on finding patterns. It is essential that pattern-finding should be given a central place in the teaching of mathematics.

(4) Peter cooperated extremely well with his two friends and gave them due credit for their part in the investigation, which continued for six months.

(5) During the course of the investigation Peter became much more mature, not only in the recording of his results, but also in his judgement of his own work. On June 1st, 1964, he wrote, 'I did this work in November 1963 but a few months later I see that there are many mistakes'. (He then gave some examples.)

(6) Peter's recording of the progress of his research (usually from day to day) gave him frequent opportunities for writing about what he was doing. His accounts were always lucid and concise; his discoveries could therefore be shared with his peers.

V. Recommendations for working with all children from 5 to 13 years

A. Courses of action

I have found that when learning mathematics all children benefit from certain courses of action.

(1) They should have opportunities to use mathematics – to see mathematics in action – so that they become aware of its potential and of why it is important to learn the subject.

(2) Children should never be taught mathematics by rote without understanding. If they understand what they are doing they are more likely to remember it and be able to use it. Moreover, less time is needed for practice if children understand and know the importance of what they are doing.

(3) Children need to learn mathematics by means of activities and investigations structured to help them to acquire specific mathematical concepts.

(4) They should use materials: simple objects from the environment as well as mathematical material such as identical squares and cubes, ten-sticks and units. Using material should be encouraged at various stages as central to the learning of mathematics – and never despised as for young children or slow learners only. Attractive materials should be available both for learning mathematics and for recording discoveries.

(5) Children should become familiar with the variety of language patterns associated with problem situations which require the use of one or more of the four operations. They should learn to use these language patterns for themselves.

(6) They should be given opportunities to talk about what they are doing, not only with their teacher but also with their peers.

(7) Teachers should be positive in their teaching of mathematics and avoid saying 'That's wrong'. If a child has arrived at a wrong answer we should ask him to tell us how he obtained it (giving him the chance to find his own mistake). Individual children need to be encouraged for every new achievement, however small.

(8) Emphasis should be placed, at all stages, on the communication of discoveries, not only in words but by pictures and by a variety of graphs.

(9) Children should be encouraged to make suggestions for various ways of doing a calculation, mental or written, and for solving problems. Their suggestions should always be welcomed and discussed.

(10) It would help the children if the mathematics teachers of the first year in the secondary school visited them in their final primary year, observing and perhaps taking an active part in the classroom. At the same time their class teachers should visit

mathematics classes in the first year of the secondary school, to see what is being done.

B. Aspects of content

(1) Older children in the age range should have a good grasp of number facts, particularly, in the first instance, of addition and subtraction facts.

(2) A record of each child's extent of number knowledge should be kept by the child as well as by the teacher. This procedure also helps children to become aware of what they are expected to memorize.

(3) Children should become aware of the central part pattern-finding has throughout the learning of mathematics.

(4) Children need to become familiar with the problem situations which require the use of one or more of the four operations for their solution. Later on, this knowledge should be extended to fractions and decimals.

(5) The scope of mathematics should be extended to include first-hand experience of all the measures, and of shapes and graphical representation.

(6) Teachers will ask how time can be made for these new topics. There are two ways in which time can be saved. Once children understand what they are doing, they need less practice to become efficient in computation. Furthermore, the easy availability of calculating machines makes it unnecessary for children to undertake written calculations in which numbers with more than three figures are involved. But understanding is more important than ever when children have to select the correct operation on a calculating machine.

Teachers should make the most of calculating machines. For example, children should be asked to check their written calculations by using machines; they should be given practice in approximation, using answers from the machine; sometimes they should be given problems to solve by machine. They should always be asked to give an approximate answer to a problem or a calculation before using the machine.

(7) Although mathematics normally has its own allocation of time, it should also be included whenever possible in general projects.

C. Change of attitude

Perhaps the most important change I hope to achieve through these suggestions is a shift in the attitude of children to mathematics. They work far more willingly at a subject which many of them inevitably find difficult if they enjoy it and can see a purpose in learning it.

D. The special case of slow learners

The most important objective for teachers of slow learners should be to change the children's attitude to mathematics. To give them confidence and to help them to enjoy mathematics, there are two essentials:

(1) to give children activities which they can do and will enjoy;
(2) to make sure that they acquire at least a minimum of number knowledge.

From the outset we should explain to them that they can always work out number facts they cannot recall from those they already know.

These children, more than any others, require encouragement for any achievement, however small.

Activities planned for slow learners should nearly always involve the use of material. It will be necessary to remind the children that everyone benefits from using material when learning mathematics, and that they are not being given material just because they find mathematics difficult.

Teachers should try to give these children a new start with fresh activities, in which they do not expect to fail. Moreover, they profit most from a programme which seems varied to them. They should not be hurried into making written recordings which they may not understand. Tape recordings could often take the place of written accounts.

Slow learners enjoy using calculating machines and gain confidence when they do so. But before they use machines they need to be familiar with the variety of situations which require the use of one of the four operations, as well as with the symbols. The promise that they will be able to use machines can act as an incentive to the children to make greater efforts.

These children also need to learn (and to use) the language patterns appropriate to problem situations in the four operations applied to number and to all the measures. Teachers should not be discouraged if this process seems to take a disproportionate amount of time. It is through acquiring confidence in using language patterns that children become able to solve everyday mathematical problems.

E. The special case of gifted children

Once again the establishment of a positive attitude to mathematics should be a priority. Some gifted children are bored because they have been made to work mainly from textbooks on content already familiar to them. Many have become so accustomed to working in this way that they regard materials as for young children or slow learners. Some prefer to work on their own and resist working with anyone else.

These children need to work with their equals, perhaps once a week, under the guidance of a teacher who is an enthusiast for mathematics. They will benefit from interchanging ideas and from taking each other's ideas further. But opportunities should also be made for them to work on their own.

However, gifted children should not be completely isolated from others in the age group. The presence of a gifted child in a mixed group can give an impetus to other children, particularly if he can be persuaded to contribute by means of suggestions or questions.

Contact with secondary schools is of major importance for these children. Their potential needs to be appreciated by those who are going to teach them. There is a danger that highly gifted children will turn away from mathematics if they are insufficiently challenged.

The provision of material is important for these children, too. They may not need to handle it, but its presence often stimulates their imagination.

These children, as well as the rest, should have a good knowledge of number facts if they are not to be handicapped when working on problems. They should be given open and sustained investigations and should be encouraged to develop these as far as possible. They should learn to present their findings in a lucid and attractive way so that other children can understand what they have done.

Children who show that they are interested in mathematics, who want to investigate problems for themselves instead of being told what to do, and who readily suggest several solutions for one calculation or problem profit from a more extensive mathematics programme than they are normally given. Examples of such a programme will be found in pages 165–176 but many others will be found in Anita Straker's book, *Mathematics for Gifted Pupils* (Longman, York: 1983).

Some children (like Peter Barnes) will want to carry out rather more academic investigations. Initially, some experience of solving directed problems will help children to become aware of wider possibilities. They should be encouraged to find investigations which interest them and to work at these over a long period until they reach a satisfactory conclusion.

F. Epilogue

Children – even slow learners – can and should take a more active part in their own learning of mathematics. However, many teachers, through no fault of their own, need more knowledge and understanding of mathematics than were provided in their education and training, if they are to help children to acquire mathematical concepts by means of structured activities.

Two recent developments should facilitate better teaching in mathematics. One was the publication of the Cockcroft Report early in 1982. Amongst its recommendations are many of those in this summary.

The second is the growing practice within LEAs of creating posts of mathematics coordinators. These teachers are promoted because they are willing to learn more mathematics, and subsequently to help their colleagues outside and inside the classroom.

Most children and students can achieve far more in mathematics than we have expected of them. But we have first to change their attitude: to make mathematics an attractive and enjoyable subject, to get them to appreciate the central part mathematics plays in work and leisure activities today, to help them both to use and to create mathematics themselves. Electronic calculators have given us the educational time to effect this change – we must not let this opportunity slip.